FILO
FANTASTIC

Mary Crownover

D1411065

TAYLOR PUBLISHING COMPANY
DALLAS, TEXAS

Designed by Deborah J. Jackson-Jones

Copyright © 1992 by Mary Crownover

Published by Taylor Publishing Company
              1550 West Mockingbird Lane
              Dallas, Texas 75235

Library of Congress Cataloging-in-Publication Data

Crownover, Mary.
      Filo fantastic / Mary Crownover.
          p.   cm.
      Includes index.
      ISBN 0-87833-810-1
      1. Cookery (Filo dough)   I. Title.
TX770.F55C76   1992
641.8—dc20   92-13584
                                    CIP

Printed in the United States of America

10   9   8   7   6   5   4   3   2   1

To my parents, Mary Frances, and Burwell Humphrey.
Thank you for sharing your love and appreciation
of good food with me.

ACKNOWLEDGMENTS

I have been overwhelmed by the enthusiasm of my friends, family, and neighbors. Thank you for the encouragement, support, and honest feedback you gave me as I created and perfected these recipes. I especially want to thank my family for being so helpful and supportive.

Thank you Barb Barman-Julius for being so helpful with all of my proofreading, and especially for being my friend.

Thank you Bev Huckaba for being a wonderful cook and loving it as much as I do—you have been a great inspiration for me over the years.

A special thank you goes to Paulette Saab, for giving me my first taste of homemade baklava; this opened the door to a new world for me.

A sincere thanks to the staff of the University of Missouri Hospital and Clinics, SameDay Surgery Center, The Eye Clinic, and Rusk Rehabilitation Center for being a wonderful test audience (my guinea pigs).

Thank you Rusty Foltz, R.D., for being my friend and offering to write a foreword for my first and second cookbooks.

CONTENTS

FOREWORD

In Mary's first book, *Cheesecake Extraordinaire*, I was honored to have the chance to share a few ideas about healthful eating and to explain how desserts like cheesecake can have a place in a well-balanced diet. I hope, in some small way, this has put cooks at ease and contributed to their enjoyment of the mouth-watering delights in *Cheesecake Extraordinaire*. I have the same advice for these recipes with filo.

Healthy eating is determined by a combination of foods, meals, and weeks—not single and absolute foods or meals. You must not look at foods as good or bad, as dietary or fattening. All food contributes to health even if that is only an emotional health (we all must treat ourselves occasionally!). It is important to remember to have a moderate and balanced diet. Eating in moderation is enjoying one serving of strudel or a filo dish rather than indulging in second and third helpings. Balance is having low-fat, high-fiber meals during the day if the filo dish you are fixing is on the high-fat, low-fiber side.

There are suggestions for lowering and modifying the fat in the recipes. However, I encourage you to prepare these appetizers, entrées, and desserts according to their recipes before modifying them so you will know how a certain dish should taste. Then you will be able to modify a recipe to suit you and your family's tastes and health needs. Again, eating a well-balanced diet will decrease or eliminate the need to modify the recipes.

Finally, if a cookbook's success is determined by the hard work, excitement, and creativity of its author, then this book should top the bestseller list. She obviously enjoys what she is doing and is totally committed to doing the best, and most thorough, job she can.

One of the comments that I have heard about her first book is the most important thing anyone can say about a cookbook... "the recipes work!" As you will see in *Filo Fantastic*, Mary works very hard to make that so.

Rusty Foltz, R.D.
Cardiopulmonary Dietitian

❖

A WORD FROM THE AUTHOR

❖❖❖

Most of us share a lifetime enthusiasm for the taste of good food, whether it is the gourmet food of today or yesterday, or the potential flavor combinations that tomorrow might bring. We simply love to indulge! I brought you *Cheesecake Extraordinaire*—a grand finale to an elegant meal. Now I am offering *Filo Fantastic*, with its sophisticated yet simple approach to cooking with filo. I hope you enjoy my recipes and my style of cooking.

Mary Crownover

GETTING STARTED: ALL ABOUT BAKING WITH FILO

HELPFUL HINTS

◆ Thoroughly read the recipe before starting. Have all of your ingredients on hand and ready to use. All of the ingredients are listed in the order that they will be used. Frequently the word "divided" will be listed after an ingredient. This simply means that the same ingredient is used at two different times in preparing the dish.

◆ A word of warning: never overstuff your filo leaves—the filling will leak out and the whole thing might tear up.

◆ When a casserole or strudel is topped with a solid sheet of filo, it is best to sprinkle a few drops of cold water over it before baking. This prevents the edges of the filo from curling up.

◆ A casserole or strudel can be made several hours ahead of time and stored in the refrigerator until it is time to bake it.

◆ A baklava-type dish or dessert, made with a nut base and with syrup poured over it, is best if made a day or so ahead of time.

◆ A hot casserole or strudel dish is best when taken right out of the oven and served immediately, while the filo is still crisp.

◆ To reheat a casserole or strudel, use a regular or conventional oven. This will restore the filo's crispness. If at all possible, do not reheat a filo casserole or strudel in a microwave—the dough will become soggy and gummy.

◆ When you are ready to work with the filo leaves, have all of your ingredients ready and plan to use a large workspace. Your workspace should be large enough to accommodate unfolded filo sheets and baking pans. You should also plan to work as quickly as possible; have a production line set up with everything in easy reach. Unfold the leaves carefully and work with 1 leaf at a time, always taking a sheet from the top of the pile to prevent the rest of the leaves from drying out and becoming brittle. If your filo becomes too dry and starts to crack while you are working with it, try misting it lightly with a little water from a clean spray bottle. Use a clean, large plastic cutting board or a smooth-finished countertop to work on. Always use a slightly dampened kitchen towel to cover the rest of the filo while you are not working with it. Too much moisture in the towel will make the filo gummy and very difficult to use. Always use plenty of melted butter when working with filo—it enhances the taste and strength of the leaves as well as the flakiness of the dough. If a leaf should tear, butter it and insert it between other leaves.

◆ The best way to cut filo leaves is with a sharp knife, sharp kitchen scissors, or a razor blade. Dull utensils will shred the dough.

◆ Cooked Toppings
All of the cooked toppings can be made in a microwave. However, be careful—overcooking will give them a rubbery texture.

◆ Freezing Casseroles and Strudels
All of the casseroles and strudels in this book freeze beautifully and can be kept in the freezer for several months. To freeze one, prepare it in the usual fashion and freeze it before baking. Or, bake the casserole or strudel and freeze it after it has cooled. It is best to wrap it in freezer-weight foil or to place it in an airtight plastic bag. Freeze the casserole or strudel without its glaze or topping; it can be added before serving time.

To thaw a casserole or strudel, place it uncovered in the refrigerator overnight or let it rest at room temperature for 2 to 3 hours.

◆ Measuring Ingredients
Accurate measurements are important. Use the back of a knife to level a measuring spoon or cup.

◆ How to Tell When a Casserole or Strudel Is Done
A dish is done when the filo is very crisp and the color is golden brown. If the dish has a custard filling, it should be set. If you are unsure whether a dish is done, turn the heat down 25° and bake the casserole or strudel a little longer (15 to 20 minutes for a large dish, 5 to 10 minutes for smaller dishes).

◆ Do not overbake a casserole or strudel—the filling will dry out. If the dish is to be served cold, let it cool on a wire rack to room temperature and then refrigerate.

INGREDIENTS

◆ Butter

For recipes and buttering pans and dishes, use fresh unsalted butter. To prevent sogginess and to have crispier filo layers, brush the layers with clarified butter. Clarified butter is simply butter with the milk solids removed. The method for clarifying butter is as follows:

> Melt the butter in a container in the microwave oven, or in a saucepan, over low heat. Remove from heat and let stand a couple of minutes. Skim the foam or bubbly mixture off the top. After it has cooled, a milky sediment will settle to the bottom. Carefully remove the remaining yellow butter solid to another dish; this is what you will brush on the sheets of filo.

If cholesterol is a problem for you, substitute an equal amount of clarified margarine for butter (the method for clarifying margarine is the same as for clarifying butter). To decrease the amount of fat in a filo dish, substitute enhanced canola oil (canola oil with a bit of butter flavoring added) for butter or margarine. See The Lighter Side of Filo for additional heart-healthy options.

◆ Cheese

Cheese is a prominent ingredient in a lot of these recipes, and it must be chosen with care. Always try to get fresh cheese. Feta is a salty cheese, so taste the filling after you have added it, or any other salty cheese, then salt the dish accordingly. When using Neufchatel cheese, you may need to increase the cooking time because it has more water in it than cream cheese, causing it to be runny if undercooked. If possible, grate your own Parmesan and Romano cheese—it is so much tastier than the packaged kind.

◆ Chocolate and Chocolate Substitutes

I recommend using real chocolate because the taste and texture are less waxlike. When milk chocolate chips are called for, you may use milk chocolate bars of an equal weight. For semisweet chocolate chips, use an equal amount of 1-ounce squares of semisweet chocolate. Melting chocolate is best accomplished in a double boiler. However, a microwave oven also works well. Start the process with dry equipment, because water causes chocolate to stiffen. Use only low heat, and stir frequently, because chocolate burns and scorches easily.

◆ Thickeners
In these recipes you can use either cornstarch or flour as a thickening agent. Cornstarch has a finer texture than flour, but any all-purpose flour will work well. Sifting flour is not necessary for any of the recipes in this book.

◆ Cream of Coconut
A very thick, extremely sweet liquid with pulp, cream of coconut is found in the beverage section of your supermarket. If you substitute cream of coconut for another ingredient, be sure to cut back on the sugar or other sweeteners the recipe calls for.

◆ Eggs
Fresh, grade A large eggs have been used in all of these recipes. However, those concerned about their cholesterol intake may substitute 2 egg whites for each whole egg a recipe calls for. But if the eggs are to be used in a custard, keep in mind that the custard will take longer to set if the yolks are omitted. To compensate, you can add cornstarch to the yolkless custard or cook the dish an additional 15 to 20 minutes.

◆ Fruit
Always use fresh fruit when it is in season.

◆ Honey
There are several types of honey available. I use liquid honey in these recipes. To prevent a honey-based syrup from becoming cloudy, add the honey after the cooking process has been completed.

◆ Kataife
Kataife (kah-ty-ee-fee) is shredded filo dough and is considered its forerunner. It is similar to shredded wheat and is used like a crust or pastry in Middle Eastern recipes. It is found in Middle Eastern or specialty food stores.

◆ Nuts
I frequently call for almonds in these recipes. Toasting them brings out the flavor and crunch that people like, and is surprisingly easy. Place the nuts evenly on a cookie sheet or baking pan, and bake for 8 to 10 minutes at 350°, stirring occasionally. When using a microwave, place the almonds in a glass pie plate and cook 5 to 7 minutes, stirring every minute until golden. Almond paste can be found in the specialty baking section at your supermarket, or you can easily make it at home. The recipe is as follows:

> Mix thoroughly ½ pound ground and blanched almonds; ½ cup sugar; and 2 egg yolks. Chill about 1 hour, or until firm. This makes 2 cups.

◆ Rose Water
Rose water is pale pink and especially fragrant. It is found in Middle Eastern or specialty food stores.

◆ Sugar
Use granulated sugar unless otherwise directed. When brown sugar is called for, always pack it tightly in the measuring cup.

◆ Filo Leaves and Strudel Dough
Filo can be found fresh in some regions of the country, in the frozen food section of your supermarket, and in the specialty or Middle Eastern food shops. It usually is found in 1-pound, long, narrow, flat boxes that contain approximately 22 to 24 sheets that are roughly 14 x 18 inches. If you are lucky and can find ½-pound boxes, this is preferred for most of the recipes in this book. In this box size, there are approximately 26 sheets that are 9 x 13 inches. Always buy filo as fresh as possible to help prevent it from becoming brittle and breaking. It will, however, keep unopened in the freezer for several months or in the refrigerator for 4 or 5 weeks. Once opened, it will keep for two weeks in the refrigerator if it is wrapped in an airtight plastic bag. Ziplock-type bags are wonderful for this. Do not refreeze opened filo; it would be too dry for use.

When thawing frozen filo, place it in the refrigerator overnight. It is best not to hurry this process, but in an emergency it can be thawed at room temperature in 2 or 3 hours. When the thawing process is rushed some or a few of the leaves will stick together. If this should happen, try to peel them apart along the edges. If you cannot separate the sheets, leave them together and use as 1 sheet, but brush it with a little extra butter.

Strudel dough is not made commercially so if you want traditional strudel pastry you must make it by hand. However, commercial filo leaves can easily be substituted when making strudel. In fact, it comes as no surprise that store-bought filo has cut into the territory of the homemade pastry world in restaurants and pastry shops. And there are other benefits—filo is predictable, it does not lose its shape, and a paper-thin sheet only contains about 30 calories.

With access to the best of both worlds—old-fashioned strudel fillings and commercially made filo—I do not see any reason for making filo by hand. In fact, it is difficult to make homemade filo because it is very time consuming, the dough is difficult to handle, and it tears easily. A professional can only produce about 10 pounds per hour. So if time is a factor and you do not want the other problems that go along with making filo, using commercially made dough is your best option.

EQUIPMENT

◆ Baking Pans
Metal pans work just as well as glass dishes for baking a casserole or strudel. It is very easy to double or cut any of these recipes in half. Just remember that if you double the quantity of the ingredients, double the size of the baking dish but **do not double the cooking time.** You may need to add 15 minutes to the baking-time. The pans in the following sizes are used in this book:

11 x 14 inch jelly roll pan	6 x 10 inch
9 x 13 inch	8 x 8 inch
7 x 11 inch	

◆ Blenders
Blenders are very useful for liquefying, purèeing, and chopping fruit. Cottage cheese is creamier after being put in a blender or food processor for a few minutes.

◆ Food Processors
A food processor or a coffee grinder comes in handy for chopping or grinding nuts.

◆ Gas or Electric Ovens
It makes no difference whether you have a gas or electric oven. However, accurate baking temperature is essential. You can easily check your cooking temperature with an oven thermometer.

◆ Kitchen Scissors
Sharp kitchen scissors are ideal for cutting filo sheets into strips or squares.

◆ Microwave Ovens
A microwave oven saves a lot of time when melting butter, toasting nuts, softening cream cheese, melting chocolate, and making toppings.

◆ Spray Bottles
A spray bottle with a fine mist works well for dampening filo sheets that have become brittle while being handled.

◆ Mixers
A heavy mixer is the one luxury that every kitchen should have. It saves time and mixes ingredients uniformly.

◆ Pastry Brushes
It is best to use a good pastry brush whenever baking with filo. Other brushes may work, but a pastry brush won't lose its bristles after extensive use.

CREATING YOUR OWN RECIPE

Creating your own recipe is fun and rewarding. It gives you the opportunity to enjoy and demonstrate your creativity. The following formula for transforming my recipes into your own creations is simple: Substitute a liquid for an equal amount of liquid, or a dry ingredient for an equal amount of a dry ingredient. This applies to fruit, fruit juices, liqueur, and extracts. Of course you may substitute sour cream for heavy cream. Nuts of any variety are interchangeable. Have fun making up your own recipes. If it sounds good to you, try it!

HISTORY OF FILO

No matter how you spell it—*phyllo, phylo, filo,* or *fillo*—the word means "leaf" in Greek. Filo (fee-lo) originated in the Far East and was adopted by the Greeks, Armenians, and other Middle Easterners. It was developed by the Turks, who first appeared around the seventh century as wandering nomads. Agriculture was their main occupation and grain was a mainstay of their diet. It is not surprising that they had a number of simple, thin, flour-based, unleavened dough recipes. One recipe, similar to a Mexican tortilla, was called *Yufkas* and was served piled in stacks with butter or other fillings between the layers. Yufkas did not evolve into the translucent filo leaf until the tenth century, after the Turks entered the Near East.

The first filo dish appears to have been baklava or "walnut strudel" and was a symbol of the good life to the Turks. When filo was first brought to other countries, its popularity was primarily limited to small, ethnic shops and restaurants and other areas where Middle Easterners congregated. As a result, its use in cooking remained limited to specific peoples for quite a while. Baklava was a secret that was difficult to keep. As "outsiders" discovered its marvelous combination of flavor and texture, with layers of delicate flaky pastry, baklava became famous and so did filo's versatility.

Should you want to make your own filo, here is a basic recipe. But be aware that filo dough can be very temperamental.

HOMEMADE FILO DOUGH

Makes 1 pound filo

4   cups all-purpose flour
½   teaspoon salt
¼   cup olive oil
2   eggs, well beaten
1   cup warm water

In a medium bowl combine the flour and salt. Mix thoroughly. Make a well in the center and put the oil and egg in it. Work this into the flour with your hands. Knead the dough until smooth and elastic, about 10 to 15 minutes. Put the dough in a greased dish, cover it, and let rise about 1 hour in a warm place.

On a covered, floured table, roll out (with a rolling pin) about ½ cup of the dough until it is very thin, about 12 inches across. Sprinkle a little more flour on the dough if needed. Flour your hands and gently put both of them under the dough. With your palms down and hands close together carefully pull it and stretch it outwardly over the backs of your hands, being careful not to tear it. Always working the dough from the center out, work your way around the table stretching in all directions. It should be very thin (transparent). Trim the edges with a sharp knife or scissors (if the edges have become crusty). Set the rolled-out sheet of pastry aside and cover with plastic wrap. Continue rolling until you have about 10 to 12 sheets, covering each with plastic wrap.

FOLDING FILO INTO SHAPES

Filo is versatile and can be shaped into many forms. After you have worked with it for a while and are comfortable handling it, try some new shapes. I have used only a few simple shapes with my recipes. Here are the directions for the folding methods used in these recipes and for a few more that aren't used in this book. Whatever shape you use, never over-fill the filo. If you try a large form you may need to lengthen the cooking time. Remember to keep the filo that you are not working with covered with a damp kitchen towel.

◆ Long Rolls

Remove one sheet of filo. (Cover the rest with a damp kitchen towel.) With a pastry brush, butter the filo with the melted butter. Layer a second and third sheet, brushing with butter. Put 1 cup of sweet filling or 1½ cups meat filling in a long row across the narrow end of the filo. Roll up jelly roll fashion. Tuck the ends underneath. Place the roll seam side down in a buttered pan. Repeat until all of the filling has been used. Brush the rolls with the remaining melted butter.

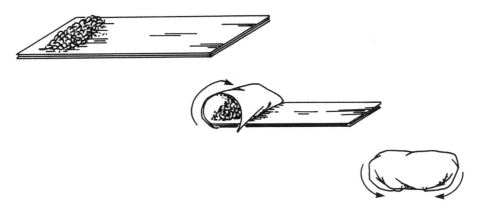

◆ Finger Rolls

Remove several sheets of filo and cut lengthwise into 2 or more sets of strips, depending on the desired width of the rolls. (Keep the filo that you are not working with covered with a damp kitchen towel.) Work with one strip at a time. Brush some of the butter on the filo with a pastry brush. Fold the strip in thirds lengthwise to make a long rectangle. Put 1 tablespoon to ¼ cup filling (depending on the size roll you desire) along the short end of the strip. Fold the sides toward the middle of the strip and roll up jelly roll fashion. Place the roll seam side down in a buttered pan. Repeat until all of the filling has been used. Brush the tops and ends with the remaining melted butter.

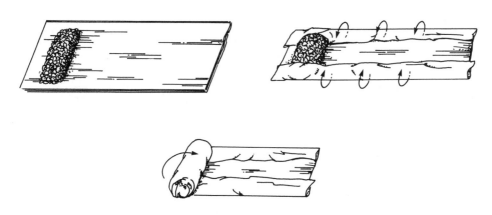

◆ Spiral Shape

Use the Long Roll directions for preparing a basic roll. Do not put as much filling in this roll as you would put in a long roll. Roll it tightly and brush with butter. Carefully fold the ends under and twist one end of the roll toward you, holding the other end, and continue twisting until the roll assumes a spiral shape. Put in a buttered pan seam side down.

◆ Horseshoe or Strudel Shape

Use the Long Roll directions for preparing a basic roll. Do not put as much filling in this roll as you would put in a long roll. Roll it tightly and brush with butter. Carefully fold the ends under and simply mold the roll into the shape of a horseshoe. Put in a buttered pan seam side down.

◆ Filo Shells

For 8 individual serving size filo shells (2½-inch standard-size muffin pan), or 16 miniature or bite-size servings (1¼-inch miniature-size muffin pan).

½ pound filo leaves, thawed   8 paper or foil muffin pan liners
½ cup butter, clarified and melted   (or 16 3-inch squares of foil)

◆

Preheat oven to 350°.

For individual serving size: Remove 3 sheets of filo. (Keep the filo that you are not working with covered with a damp kitchen towel.) Using sharp scissors or a sharp knife cut each removed pastry sheet, into 4 5-inch squares. Brush butter on 3

squares of filo with a pastry brush and place them on top of each other. Place a
liner in a muffin cup, then gently mold the buttered pastry squares into the cup,
leaving a 1-inch overhang. Repeat the process to form the desired number of pastry
shells.

For miniature serving size: Follow the above instructions, but cut each of the 3
sheets into 6 3-inch squares and line the miniature muffin pans with foil by molding
a square into each cup.

Bake shells at 350° for 10 minutes, or until they are crisp and golden brown. Place
the muffin pan on a wire rack to cool for 10 minutes before filling the shells.
Remove the liners before serving. Serve immediately after filling.

Note: Muffin liners add additional support while handling filo shells. Use the liners
until you are comfortable handling the filo without them.

◆ Triangles
Cut a sheet of filo lengthwise into the desired width. (I usually cut a sheet into
thirds or fourths lengthwise.) You will have 3 or 4 narrow strips or rectangles. Take 2
strips of filo and lay one on top of the other. Brush some of the butter on the top
strip with a pastry brush. Put the filling in the center, about 1 inch from the end of
the strip. Put about 1 tablespoon to ¼ cup of filling on the strip, depending on the
size or width; use more for a wider strip, or larger triangle. Fold the end of the strip
up over the filling to form a little envelope that just covers the filling. Then swing
the left corner over to meet the opposite edge and form a triangle. Bring the right

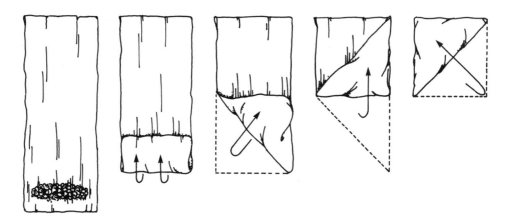

corner straight up, (as if you were folding a flag) to form a triangle. Swing the bottom right corner up to meet the opposite edge. Continue folding the triangle as directed until all of the filo strip has been folded. Butter the outside of the triangle and put it seam side down in the buttered pan. Continue until all of the ingredients have been used.

TANTALIZING
APPETIZERS

SMOKED SAUSAGE AND CHEESE BITES

Makes 20 to 25

1 pound smoked sausage	½ pound filo leaves, thawed and covered with a damp kitchen towel
1 cup of your favorite barbecue sauce	
½ cup onion, chopped	½ cup butter, clarified and melted
12 ounces cheddar cheese, grated	

Butter a 9 × 13-inch pan; set aside. Preheat oven to 350°.

Peel the casing off of the sausage and slice into thin slices, about ½-inch thick. Set aside. Put the barbecue sauce in a small bowl and stir in the onion. Set aside.

Lay several sheets of filo on a large plastic cutting board. Cut the sheets lengthwise into 2 sets of strips. Work with one strip at a time. Fold each strip in thirds lengthwise to form a long rectangle. Brush some of the butter on the filo with a pastry brush. Put a slice of sausage in the center of one end of the rectangle. Put a teaspoon of barbecue sauce on the sausage. Top with about 1 teaspoon cheese. Fold the edges over the filling, encasing it, and roll up jelly roll fashion. Place the little roll seam side down on the buttered pan. Repeat to form additional rolls until all of the filling has been used, placing each little roll next to the previous one. Brush the tops and ends with the remaining melted butter.

Bake at 350° for 40 to 50 minutes, or until the filo is crisp and golden brown. Serve hot.

CRAB AND MUSHROOM STRUDEL

Makes 16 to 20

1 bunch green onions, chopped	½ cup fresh parsley, chopped
2 pounds fresh mushrooms, sliced	¼ cup white wine
½ cup butter	salt and pepper
1 pound crab meat (fresh, canned, or frozen)	cayenne pepper
1 pound cream cheese, at room temperature	1 pound filo leaves, thawed and covered with a damp kitchen towel
4 ounces fresh Romano cheese, grated	1 cup butter, clarified and melted
4 ounces fresh Parmesan cheese, grated	2 cups bread crumbs, toasted

Butter a 9 × 13-inch pan; set aside. Preheat oven to 350°.

In a large skillet, over low heat, cook the green onions and mushrooms in the butter until partially done (ingredients should still be firm). Add the crab and continue cooking a few more minutes until all of the ingredients are heated throughout. Drain well and set aside.

In a large bowl combine the cream cheese, Romano cheese, and Parmesan cheese. Stir in the parsley and wine, mixing well. Add the ingredients from the skillet. Add salt, pepper, and cayenne to taste and mix thoroughly.

Lay 1 sheet of filo on a large plastic cutting board. Brush some of the butter on the filo with a pastry brush. Layer a second and a third sheet of filo on top, brushing each one with butter. Sprinkle about ⅓ cup bread crumbs on the filo. Put 1½ cups of the crab mixture in a long row across the narrow end of the filo. Roll up jelly roll fashion and tuck the ends underneath. Place seam side down in the buttered pan. Repeat to form additional rolls until all of the crab has been used, placing each roll next to the previous one. Brush the tops and ends with the remaining melted butter.

Bake at 350° for 40 to 50 minutes, or until the filo is crisp and golden brown. Cut the rolls diagonally before serving. Serve hot.

VIDALIA ONION BAKE

◆

Makes 20 to 24

2	Vidalia onions, chopped in chunks	1	ounce Parmesan cheese, grated
1	green pepper, chopped in chunks	2	eggs
3	garlic cloves, minced	4	yolks
½	cup fresh parsley, chopped		salt and pepper
8	ounces water chestnuts, drained	1	teaspoon celery salt
1	envelope (1.4 ounces) dry vegetable soup mix	½	pound filo leaves, thawed and covered with a damp kitchen towel
24	ounces cream cheese, at room temperature	½	cup butter, clarified and melted
½	pound feta cheese, crumbled		

◆

Butter a 9 × 13-inch pan; set aside. Preheat oven to 350°.

Put onions in a food processor and process until somewhat chopped. Add the green pepper, garlic, parsley, and water chestnuts and process until finely chopped. Drain well and set aside.

In a large mixing bowl combine the soup mix and cream cheese. Beat with an electric mixer until blended. Stir in the feta and Parmesan cheese. Beat in the eggs and egg yolks. Add salt and pepper to taste and celery salt. Stir the onion mixture into the cream cheese. Mix thoroughly and set aside.

Place 1 sheet of filo in the bottom of the buttered pan, folding it to fit. Brush some of the butter on the filo with a pastry brush. Layer a second and a third sheet of filo on top, folding them to fit and brushing each one with butter. Spread the cream cheese and onion mixture over the filo. Top with 4 or 5 sheets of folded, buttered filo. Before baking, sprinkle a few drops of water over the top and around the edges of the filo to prevent it from curling.

Bake at 350° for 40 to 50 minutes, or until the filo is crisp and golden brown. Serve hot.

SPICY JAMBALAYA STRUDEL

◆

Makes 24 2-inch appetizers

¼ cup margarine
2 tablespoons olive oil
½ pound Italian or Polish sausage, cut into thin slices
2 chicken breast halves, skinned, boned, and cut into narrow strips
1 pound shrimp, peeled and deveined
1 onion, chopped
1 bunch green onions, chopped
2 garlic cloves, minced
1 green pepper, chopped
1 stalk celery, chopped
8 ounces mushrooms, sliced
2 tablespoons fresh parsley, chopped
½ teaspoon chili powder
½ teaspoon thyme

2 teaspoons lemon juice
¼ cup white wine
30 ounces Cajun-style stewed tomatoes, drained
 salt and pepper
 cayenne pepper
1 tablespoon cornstarch
¼ cup water
2 cups bread crumbs (or 2 cups cooked rice), toasted
1 pound filo leaves, thawed and covered with a damp kitchen towel
1 cup butter, clarified and melted

◆

Butter a 9 × 13-inch pan; set aside. Preheat oven to 350°.

Melt the margarine over medium-low heat in a large skillet. Add the olive oil and heat until hot. Add the sausage, chicken, shrimp, onions, garlic, green pepper, celery, and mushrooms, cooking and stirring until partially done (ingredients should still be firm and meat should be slightly pink). Stir in the parsley, chili powder, thyme, lemon juice, and wine. Stir in the tomatoes and add salt, pepper, and cayenne to taste. Mix thoroughly, remove from the heat, and set aside.

Drain the juice from the skillet into a small saucepan. Put the cornstarch and water in a small cup and stir until the cornstarch dissolves; stir this mixture into the juice. Stir while cooking over low heat, until thickened. Stir the juice into the jambalaya filling and mix thoroughly.

Place 1 sheet of filo in the bottom of the buttered pan, folding it to fit. Brush some of the butter on the filo with a pastry brush. Layer a second and a third sheet of filo on top, folding them to fit and brushing each one with butter. Put the bread crumbs (or cooked rice) on the filo. Put the jambalaya filling on the bread crumbs spreading it out evenly. Top with 5 or 6 sheets of folded, buttered filo. Before baking, sprinkle a few drops of water over the top and around the edges of the filo to prevent it from curling.

Bake at 350° for 40 to 50 minutes, or until the filo is crisp and golden brown. Serve hot.

FILO-WRAPPED
ITALIAN SAUSAGE LINKS

◆

Makes 12

¼ cup margarine
2 pounds Italian sausage links, cut
    in half lengthwise
1 small onion, chopped
    spicy mustard
    barbecue sauce

½ pound filo leaves, thawed and
    covered with a damp kitchen
    towel
½ cup butter, clarified and melted
6 ounces extra-sharp cheddar
    cheese, grated

◆

Butter a 7 × 11-inch pan; set aside. Preheat oven to 350°.

Melt the margarine over medium-low heat in a medium skillet. Cook the sausage and onion until partially done (onion should still be firm and meat should be slightly pink) and drain well. Remove and set aside.

Lay 1 sheet of filo on a large plastic cutting board. Brush some of the butter on the filo with a pastry brush. Layer a second and a third sheet of filo on top, brushing each one with butter. Spread a thin layer of mustard on the filo. Spread a layer of barbecue sauce over the mustard. Place half of the sausage across the narrow end of the filo. Sprinkle half of the onion on the sausage. Sprinkle half of the cheese on and roll up jelly roll fashion. Tuck the ends underneath. Place the roll seam side down in the buttered pan. Repeat to form another roll, placing it next to the previous one. Brush the tops and ends with the butter.

Bake at 350° for 40 to 50 minutes, or until the filo is crisp and golden. Cut the rolls diagonally before serving. Serve hot. Serve with extra barbecue sauce at the table, if desired.

CRAB AND CHEESE BITES

◆

Makes 20 to 25

8	ounces cream cheese, at room temperature	½	pound filo leaves, thawed and covered with a damp kitchen towel
4	ounces Parmesan cheese, grated	½	cup butter, clarified and melted
6	ounces crab meat, picked over	1	ounce Parmesan cheese, grated
4	ounces canned mushrooms, sliced		
½	cup onion, chopped		
2	egg yolks		
½	cup walnuts, chopped		
	salt and pepper		
	cayenne pepper		

◆

Butter a 9 × 13-inch pan; set aside. Preheat oven to 350°.

In a medium mixing bowl combine the cream cheese, Parmesan cheese, crab meat, mushrooms, onion, and egg yolks. Beat with an electric mixer until thoroughly mixed. Stir in the walnuts. Add salt, pepper, and cayenne to taste. Set aside.

Lay several sheets of filo on a large plastic cutting board. Cut the sheets, lengthwise, into 2 sets of strips. Work with one strip at a time. Fold each strip in thirds lengthwise to form a long rectangle. Brush some of the butter on the filo with a pastry brush. Put 1 heaping tablespoon of the crab and cheese mixture in the center of one end of the rectangle. Fold the filo in thirds (lengthwise) again by folding the edges over the filling, encasing it, and rolling the filo in jelly roll fashion. Place the roll seam side down on the buttered pan. Repeat to form additional rolls until all of the filling has been used, placing each roll next to the previous one. Brush the tops and ends with the remaining melted butter. Sprinkle a little cayenne and the remaining Parmesan cheese on top.

Bake at 350° for 40 to 50 minutes, or until the filo is crisp and golden brown. Serve hot.

CAYENNE AND CRAB SQUARES

◆

Makes 24 2-inch appetizers

2	egg yolks	½	pound filo leaves, thawed and covered with a damp kitchen towel
8	ounces cream cheese, at room temperature		
3	green onions, chopped	½	cup butter, clarified and melted
6	ounces chili sauce	6	ounces crab meat (fresh or canned), cooked and picked over
1	tablespoon cornstarch horseradish cayenne pepper		

◆

Butter a 9 × 13-inch pan; set aside. Preheat oven to 350°.

Beat the egg yolks in a bowl, add the cream cheese and onion and mix thoroughly. Set aside.

In a small bowl combine the chili sauce, cornstarch, horseradish, and cayenne. Set aside.

Lay 2 sheets of filo on a large plastic cutting board. Cut the sheets, lengthwise, into 2 sets of strips. Work with 1 strip at a time. Fold a strip lengthwise, in thirds to form a long rectangle. Brush some of the butter on the filo with a pastry brush. Put 1 tablespoon of cream cheese mixture in the center of one end of the rectangle. Put 2 teaspoons of chili sauce on top of the cream cheese. Put 2 teaspoons of crab over the chili sauce. Again fold the filo in thirds lengthwise, by folding the edges over the filling, encasing it, and roll up jelly roll fashion. Place the roll seam side down on the buttered pan. Repeat to form additional rolls until all the filling is used, placing each roll next to the previous one. Brush the tops and ends with the remaining melted butter.

Bake at 350° for 40 to 50 minutes, or until the filo is crisp and golden brown. Cool completely on wire rack, then chill uncovered for a couple of hours. Serve cold.

Note: This appetizer can be made a day ahead.

CURRY CHICKEN BITES

◆

Makes 24 2-inch appetizers

3 cups cooked chicken, cubed	¾ cup coconut, grated, divided
16 ounces cream cheese, at room temperature	¾ cup almonds, toasted and sliced, divided
8 ounces sour cream	½ cup fresh parsley, chopped
3 egg yolks, beaten	½ pound filo leaves, thawed and covered with a damp kitchen towel
1 onion, chopped	
1 green pepper, chopped	
2 tablespoons Worcestershire sauce	½ cup butter, clarified and melted
1 tablespoon sugar	
2 teaspoons garlic powder	
2 tablespoons curry powder	
salt and pepper	

◆

Butter a 9 × 13-inch pain; set aside. Preheat oven to 350°.

Beat the chicken, cream cheese, sour cream, and egg yolks in a large bowl with an electric mixer. Add the onion, green pepper, Worcestershire sauce, sugar, garlic, and curry powder. Add salt and pepper to taste. Add ½ cup coconut, ½ cup almonds, and the parsley and mix thoroughly. Set aside.

Place 1 sheet of filo in the bottom of the buttered pan, folding it to fit. Brush some of the butter on the filo with a pastry brush. Layer a second and a third sheet of folded, buttered filo. Spread the mixture evenly over the filo. Top with 2 or 3 sheets of folded, buttered filo. Sprinkle the remaining coconut and almonds on top. Before baking, sprinkle a few drops of water over the top and around the edges of the filo to prevent it from curling.

Bake at 350° for 40 to 50 minutes, or until the filo is crisp and golden brown. Serve hot or cold.

CAJUN ROLL-UPS

Makes 10 to 12

½ cup margarine
4 chicken breast halves, skinned, boned and cubed
1 pound shrimp, peeled and deveined
1 onion, chopped
1 green pepper, chopped
1 garlic clove, minced
½ cup black olives, chopped
    salt and pepper
    cayenne pepper

12 ounces bottled Cajun-style barbecue sauce
1 pound filo leaves, thawed and covered with a damp kitchen towel
1 cup butter, clarified and melted

◆

Butter a 9 × 13-inch pain; set aside. Preheat oven to 350°.

Melt the margarine in a large skillet over medium-low heat. Cook the chicken, shrimp, onion, green pepper, and garlic until partially done (ingredients should still be firm and meat should be slightly pink). Drain well. Stir in the olives and add salt, pepper, and cayenne pepper to taste. Stir in the barbecue sauce and set aside.

Lay 1 sheet of filo on a large plastic cutting board. Brush some of the butter on the filo with a pastry brush. Layer with a second and a third sheet of filo on top, brushing each one with butter. Put 1½ cups of the chicken mixture in a long row across the narrow end of the filo. Roll jelly roll fashion. Tuck the ends underneath. Place seam side down in the buttered pan. Repeat to form additional rolls until all of the filling has been used, placing each roll next to the previous one. Brush the tops and ends with remaining melted butter.

Bake at 350° for 40 to 50 minutes, or until the filo is crisp and golden brown. Cut the rolls diagonally before serving. Serve hot.

BEST-OF-ITALY POCKETS

◆

Makes 16 to 20

2	pounds Italian sausage	1	tablespoon sugar
2	eggs, beaten		salt and pepper
1	cup bread crumbs	8	ounces Romano cheese, grated
1	cup flour	1	pound filo leaves, thawed and covered with a damp kitchen towel
½	cup olive oil		
1	stick margarine		
1	onion, chopped	1	cup butter, clarified and melted
2	garlic cloves, minced		
1	green pepper, chopped		
¼	cup fresh parsley, chopped		
8	ounces tomato paste		
15	ounces Italian-style tomato sauce		
1	teaspoon basil		
1	teaspoon oregano		

◆

Butter a 9 × 13-inch pain; set aside. Preheat oven to 350°.

Combine the sausage, eggs, and bread crumbs in a medium bowl. Mix thoroughly and form into 1- or 2-inch balls. Put the flour in a small bowl and coat the meatballs in it. In a large skillet heat the olive oil over low heat. Cook the meatballs in the oil until partially done (meat should be slightly pink). Remove from skillet and set aside. Wipe the skillet clean.

Melt the margarine over low heat in the skillet and cook the onion, garlic, and green pepper for a couple of minutes or until partially done (ingredients should still be firm). Add the parsley, tomato paste, and sauce. Stir in the basil, oregano, and sugar. Add salt and pepper to taste. Stir in the meatballs and mix completely.

Lay 1 sheet of filo on a large plastic cutting board. Brush some of the butter on the filo with a pastry brush. Layer a second and a third sheet of filo on top, brushing each with butter. Spoon a row of meatballs and sauce along the narrow edge of the filo. Sprinkle about ½ cup of the cheese over the meatball mixture. Roll up jelly roll fashion. Tuck the ends underneath. Place the roll seam side down in the buttered pan. Repeat to form additional rolls until all of the filling has been used, placing each roll next to the previous one. Brush the tops and ends with the remaining melted butter. Sprinkle the remaining cheese on top.

Bake at 350° for 40 to 50 minutes, or until the filo is crisp and golden brown. Cut the rolls diagonally before serving. Serve hot.

Note: If not to be served the same day, cover well, and freeze. Thaw at room temperature for a few hours. Reheat at 350° for 30 to 45 minutes.

SEAFOOD PEPPER BITES

◆

Makes 25

12 ounces cream cheese, at room temperature	salt and pepper
¼ cup mayonnaise	cayenne pepper
¼ cup fresh parsley, chopped	½ pound filo leaves, thawed and covered with a damp kitchen towel
3 green onions, chopped	
3 egg yolks	½ cup butter, clarified and melted
4 ounces crab meat, cooked	
¼ pound shrimp, cooked, peeled and chopped	

◆

Butter a 9 × 13-inch pan; set aside. Preheat oven to 350°.

Beat the cream cheese, mayonnaise, parsley, green onions, and egg yolks in a medium mixing bowl with an electric mixer until thoroughly mixed. Stir in the crab and shrimp. Add salt, pepper, and cayenne to taste. Set aside.

Lay several sheets of filo on a large plastic cutting board. Cut the sheets, lengthwise, into 2 sets of strips. Work with one strip at a time. Fold a strip in thirds lengthwise to form a long rectangle. Brush some of the butter on the filo with a pastry brush. Put 1 heaping tablespoon of the mixture in the center of one end of the rectangle. Fold the filo again in thirds (lengthwise) by folding the edges over the filling, encasing it, and rolling the filo in a jelly roll fashion. Place the roll seam side down on the buttered pan. Repeat to form additional rolls until all of the filling has been used, placing each roll next to the previous one. Brush the tops and ends with the remaining melted butter. Sprinkle a little cayenne on top.

Bake at 350° for 40 to 50 minutes, or until the filo is crisp and golden brown. Serve hot or cold.

PORK TENDERLOIN AND MUSHROOM STRUDEL

Makes 16 to 20

1½	pounds pork tenderloin	5	ounces fresh Romano cheese, grated
½	cup butter		
1	medium onion, chopped	4	teaspoons all-purpose Greek seasoning
2	garlic cloves, minced		
1	pound mushrooms, thinly sliced salt and pepper	1	pound filo leaves, thawed and covered with a damp kitchen towel
2	cups sour cream		
1	pound Swiss cheese, grated	1	cup butter, clarified and melted
4	ounces fresh Parmesan cheese, grated		

Butter a 9 × 13-inch pan; set aside. Preheat oven to 350°.

Slice the pork tenderloin into thin strips. Melt the butter in a large skillet over low heat. Add the pork, onion, and garlic, cook until partially done (ingredients should still be firm and meat should be slightly pink). Remove from the skillet and put in a medium bowl. Cook the mushrooms in the skillet for a couple of minutes, until partially done. Remove from skillet and add to the pork mixture. Add salt and pepper to taste. Set aside.

Put the sour cream in a large bowl and stir in the Swiss, Parmesan, and Romano cheeses, mixing thoroughly. Stir in the Greek seasoning. Add the meat, onion, and mushroom mixture and mix thoroughly.

Lay 1 sheet of filo on a large plastic cutting board. Brush some of the butter on the filo with a pastry brush. Layer a second and a third sheet of filo on top, brushing each one with butter. Put 1½ cups of the filling in a long row at the narrow end of the filo. Roll jelly roll fashion. Tuck the ends underneath. Place seam side down in the buttered pan. Repeat to form additional rolls until all of the filling has been used, placing each roll next to the previous one. Brush the tops and ends with the remaining melted butter.

Bake at 350° for 40 to 50 minutes, or until the filo is crisp and golden brown. Cut the rolls diagonally before serving. Serve hot.

Note: If not to be served that day, cover well, and freeze. Thaw at room temperature for a couple of hours. Reheat at 350° for 30 to 45 minutes.

CHINESE CHICKEN ROLLS WITH PLUM SAUCE

◆

Makes 20 to 24

3 cups chicken, cooked and cubed	1 cup butter, clarified and melted
1 bunch green onions, chopped	1 cup hoisin sauce*
8 ounces canned mushrooms, sliced	
8 ounces water chestnuts, sliced	***Plum Sauce***
½ medium head of cabbage, shredded	1 cup plum jam
	2 tablespoons sherry
¾ cup almonds, coarsely chopped	1 tablespoon vinegar
2 garlic cloves, minced	2 teaspoons chili powder
1 tablespoon sesame oil	½ teaspoon ginger
soy sauce	2 garlic cloves, minced
pepper	
1 pound filo leaves, thawed and covered with a damp kitchen towel	

◆

Butter a 9 × 13-inch pan; set aside. Preheat oven to 350°.

Put the chicken into a large bowl and add the onions, mushrooms, and water chestnuts. Add the cabbage, almonds, garlic, and sesame oil and mix thoroughly. Stir in soy sauce and pepper to taste; mix thoroughly.

Lay 1 sheet of filo on a large plastic cutting board. Brush some of the butter on the filo with a pastry brush. Layer a second and a third sheet of filo on top, brushing each one with butter. Spread a thin layer of hoisin sauce on the filo. Put 1½ cups of the chicken mixture in a long row across narrow end of the filo. Roll up jelly roll fashion. Tuck the ends underneath. Place seam side down in the buttered pan. Repeat to form additional rolls until all of the chicken filling has been used, placing each roll next to the previous one. Brush the tops and ends with melted butter.

Bake at 350° for 40 to 50 minutes, or until the filo is crisp and golden brown. Cut the rolls diagonally before serving. Serve hot with the Plum Sauce.

Plum Sauce
In a medium bowl combine the plum jam, sherry, vinegar, chili powder, ginger, and garlic. Serve sauce at room temperature. Store in the refrigerator.

*Hoisin sauce can be found in the Asian foods section of your grocery store.

FILO-WRAPPED SWEET AND SOUR MEATBALLS

Makes 16 to 20

2	pounds ground chuck hamburger	½	cup margarine
2	eggs, beaten	8	ounces chili sauce
2	cups bread crumbs	12	ounces grape jelly
1	onion, chopped	2	tablespoons cornstarch
⅓	cup soy sauce	1	pound filo leaves, thawed and covered with a damp kitchen towel
1	envelope (1.4 ounces) dry onion soup mix		
	salt and pepper	1	cup butter, clarified and melted

Butter a 9 × 13-inch pain; set aside. Preheat oven to 350°.

Combine the hamburger, eggs, bread crumbs, onion, soy sauce, and onion soup mix in a large bowl. Add salt and pepper to taste and mix thoroughly. Roll the meat mixture into 2-inch balls and place on a cookie sheet.

Melt the margarine in a large skillet over low heat. Cook the meatballs until barely done (meat should be slightly pink). Drain meat and return to the cookie sheet. Set aside.

In a medium bowl thoroughly combine the chili sauce, grape jelly, and cornstarch.

Lay 1 sheet of filo on a large plastic cutting board. Brush some of the butter on the filo with a pastry brush. Layer a second and a third sheet of filo on top brushing each one with butter. Spoon on a small row of meatballs along the narrow edge of the filo. Put about ¼ cup of sauce over the meatballs. Roll up jelly roll fashion. Tuck the ends underneath. Place the roll seam side down in the buttered pan. Repeat to form additional rolls until all the meatballs have been used, placing each roll next to the previous ones. Brush the tops and ends with remaining melted butter. Cut the top layers of the filo diagonally before baking. Spoon on the remaining sweet and sour sauce.

Bake at 350° for 30 to 40 minutes, or until the filo is crisp and golden brown. Serve hot.

CHICKEN RANGOON WITH SWEET AND SOUR SAUCE

◆

Makes 10 to 12

2 cups cooked chicken, skinned, boned, and cubed	***Sweet and Sour Sauce***
1 bunch green onions, chopped	12 ounces apricot preserves
2 tablespoons sesame oil	2 tablespoons pineapple juice
16 ounces cream cheese, at room temperature	1 garlic clove, minced
salt and white pepper	1 teaspoon ginger
1 pound filo leaves, thawed and covered with a damp kitchen towel	soy sauce
1 cup butter, clarified and melted	

◆

Butter a 9 × 13-inch pan; set aside. Preheat oven to 350°.

Combine the chicken, green onions, sesame oil, and cream cheese in a large bowl. Add salt and pepper to taste and mix thoroughly.

Lay 1 sheet of filo on a large plastic cutting board. Brush some of the butter on the filo with a pastry brush. Across the narrow end of the filo, put 1 cup of filling mixture in the center on the bottom edge. Fold the sides of the filo over the mixture, encasing it, and roll up jelly roll fashion. Place seam side down on the buttered sheet. Repeat to form additional rolls until all of the filling has been used, placing each roll next to the previous one. Brush the rolls with the remaining melted butter.

Bake at 350° for 40 to 50 minutes, or until the filo is crisp and golden brown. Serve hot with soy sauce, if desired, and sweet and sour sauce.

Sweet and Sour Sauce
Combine the apricot preserves, pineapple juice, garlic, and ginger in a medium bowl and mix thoroughly. Serve sauce at room temperature. Any leftover sauce should be refrigerated.

SOUTHWESTERN BAKE

◆

Makes 16 to 20

3	pound pork roast, well trimmed	2	jalapeños, rinsed, seeded and chopped
6	tablespoons chili powder		
3	cups water	5	eggs
¼	cup oil	10	ounces salsa
6	ounces tomato paste		salt and pepper
1	teaspoon cayenne pepper	½	pound filo leaves, thawed and covered with a damp kitchen towel
2	garlic cloves, minced		
1½	teaspoons salt		
1	teaspoon oregano	½	cup butter, clarified and melted
¼	teaspoon cumin	8	ounces mozzarella cheese, grated
½	teaspoon coriander	8	ounces Monterey Jack cheese, grated
1	onion, chopped		
1	green pepper, chopped		sour cream (optional)
1	red pepper, chopped		
½	cup margarine		
8	ounces green chilies, rinsed and seeded		

◆

Butter a 9 × 13-inch pan; set aside. Preheat oven to 350°.

Place the trimmed pork roast in a Dutch oven. In a medium bowl, combine the chili powder and water. Stir in the oil, tomato paste, cayenne, garlic, salt, oregano, cumin, and coriander and mix thoroughly. Pour the marinade over the meat, cover, and cook for 4 hours, or until done. Remove from oven and pour off the marinade. Cover the meat and let it cool. When cool, cut into bite-size pieces, cover, and set aside. (The meat can be prepared the day before or it can be cooked in a Crock-pot on low for about 8 hours.)

In a medium skillet over medium heat, cook the onion and peppers in the margarine for a couple of minutes, or until partially done (ingredients should still be firm); drain well. Stir the green chilies and jalapeños into the onion mixture. Set aside. Beat the eggs in a bowl, stir in the salsa, and combine thoroughly. Add the salt and pepper to taste. Set aside.

Place 1 sheet of filo in the bottom of the buttered pan, folding it to fit. Brush some of the butter on the filo with a pastry brush. Layer a second and a third sheet of folded, buttered filo on top. Evenly distribute the meat over the filo. Spread the onion mixture over the meat. Sprinkle the mozzarella and Monterey Jack cheese over the onions. Pour the egg mixture over the cheese. Top with 4 or 5 sheets of folded, buttered filo. Before baking, sprinkle a few drops of water over the top and around the edges of the filo to prevent it from curling.

Bake at 350° for 40 to 50 minutes, or until the filling is set and the filo is crisp and golden brown. Serve hot with a tablespoon of sour cream on top, if desired.

ANTIPASTO ROLL-UPS

◆

Makes 8 to 10

6	slices salami	½	cup green pepper, chopped
½	cup pepperoni	½	cup fresh parsley, chopped
½	pound filo leaves, thawed and covered with a damp kitchen towel	½	cup canned mushrooms, sliced and drained
		½	cup black olives, sliced
½	cup butter, clarified and melted	4	ounces mozzarella cheese, grated
1	cup pizza sauce	2	ounces Parmesan cheese, grated
1	cup onion, chopped		

◆

Butter a 9 × 13-inch pan; set aside. Preheat oven to 350°.

If the salami and pepperoni are not cut into *thin* slices, cut into thin strips ¼-inch wide and set aside.

Lay 1 sheet of filo on a large plastic cutting board. Brush some of the butter on the filo with a pastry brush. Layer a second, third, and fourth sheet on top, brushing each one with butter. Spread the pizza sauce over the filo. Sprinkle the onion, green pepper, and parsley over the sauce. Sprinkle the mushrooms and olives on. Arrange the salami and pepperoni evenly over the pizza. Sprinkle the cheeses evenly over the pizza. Using the long edge of the filo, carefully roll it up in a jelly roll fashion. Tuck the ends underneath. Place the roll seam side down in the buttered pan. Brush the top and ends with the remaining melted butter.

Bake at 350° for 40 to 50 minutes, or until the filo is crisp and golden brown. Cut the roll diagonally before serving. Serve hot.

Note: This recipe can easily be doubled.

GYRO ROLLS WITH YOGURT SAUCE

◆

Makes 16 to 20

Yogurt Sauce

1   pint yogurt, plain
1   cucumber, peeled and seeded
2   garlic cloves, minced
½   onion, chopped
2   tablespoons olive oil
1   tablespoon lemon juice
     salt and pepper

3   pounds beef loin or lamb, boned
       and well trimmed
1   cup olive oil
2   tablespoons lemon juice
1   onion, chopped

4   garlic cloves, minced
2   teaspoons oregano
3   bay leaves
2   teaspoons all-purpose Greek
       seasoning
     salt and pepper
1   pound filo leaves, thawed and
       covered with a damp kitchen
       towel
1   cup butter, clarified and melted
1   onion, thinly sliced
2   tomatoes, chopped
½   cup black olives, sliced
1   green pepper, chopped

◆

Yogurt Sauce

In a small bowl, combine the yogurt, cucumber, garlic, onion, olive oil, lemon juice, and salt and pepper to taste. Put the mixture in a blender or food processor and blend thoroughly. Return to the bowl and refrigerate over night.

Cut the meat into 1½-inch cubes. Place in a medium bowl. Combine the olive oil, lemon juice, onion, garlic, oregano, bay leaves, Greek seasoning, and salt and pepper in a small bowl and mix thoroughly. Pour the marinade over the meat and refrigerate over night.

Butter a 9 × 13-inch pan; set aside. Preheat oven to 350°.

Place the meat and marinade in a Dutch oven. Cover and cook for 3 hours, or until done. Remove from oven and pour off the marinade. Cover the meat and set aside. The meat can be cooked in a Crock-pot on low for about 6 hours.

Lay 1 sheet of filo on a large plastic cutting board. Brush some of the butter on the filo with a pastry brush. Layer a second and a third sheet of filo on top, brushing each one with butter. Put about 1½ cups of the meat in a long row at the narrow end of the filo. Put several tablespoons of the yogurt sauce over the meat. Layer a few slices of onion and some chopped tomato, olives, and green pepper over the meat. Roll up jelly roll fashion. Tuck the ends underneath. Place the roll seam side down on the buttered pan. Repeat to form additional rolls until all the filling has been used, placing each roll next to the previous one. Brush the tops and ends with the melted butter.

Bake at 350° for 40 to 50 minutes, or until the filo is crisp and golden brown. Cut the rolls diagonally before serving. Serve hot with the yogurt sauce.

BLUE CHEESE BITES

◆

Makes 20 to 25

8 ounces cream cheese, at room temperature	salt and pepper
5 ounces blue cheese	cayenne pepper
½ cup fresh parsley, chopped	½ pound filo leaves, thawed and covered with a damp kitchen
½ cup onion, chopped	towel
2 egg yolks	½ cup butter, clarified and melted
½ cup walnuts, chopped	

◆

Butter a 9 × 13-inch pan; set aside. Preheat oven to 350°.

Combine the cream cheese, blue cheese, parsley, onion, and egg yolks in a medium mixing bowl. Beat with an electric mixer until thoroughly mixed. Stir in the walnuts. Add salt, pepper, and cayenne to taste. Set aside.

Lay several sheets of filo on a large plastic cutting board. Cut the sheets, lengthwise, into 2 sets of strips. Work with 1 strip at a time. Fold each strip lengthwise in thirds to form a long rectangle. Brush some of the butter on the filo with a pastry brush. Put 1 heaping tablespoon of the cream cheese mixture in the center of one end of the rectangle. Fold the filo in thirds (lengthwise) again by folding the edges over the filling, encasing it, and roll the filo in jelly roll fashion. Place the roll seam side down on the buttered pan. Repeat to form additional rolls until all the filling has been used, placing each roll next to the previous one. Brush the tops and ends with the remaining melted butter. Sprinkle a little cayenne on top.

Bake at 350° for 40 to 50 minutes, or until the filo is crisp and golden brown. Serve hot.

❖❖❖

BARBECUED BRISKET BITES

◆

Makes 16 to 20

2 to 3 pounds beef brisket
1 tablespoon liquid smoke
2 tablespoons soy sauce
1 envelope (1.4 ounces) onion soup
    mix
1 cup water
1 stick margarine
1 onion, chopped
1 green pepper, chopped
1 garlic clove, minced

2 tablespoons cornstarch
18 ounces barbecue sauce
    salt and pepper
1 pound filo leaves, thawed and
    covered with a damp kitchen
    towel
1½ cups butter, clarified and melted

◆

Butter a 9 × 13-inch pan; set aside. Preheat oven to 350°.

Put the brisket in a medium roasting pan. Put the liquid smoke, soy sauce, and onion soup on the brisket. Add the water and cover tightly with foil. Bake at 350° for 3 hours or until done. Remove from pan and set aside to cool.

Melt margarine in a large skillet over medium heat. Cook the onion, green pepper, and garlic until they are still firm and partially done. Drain well. Stir in the cornstarch and barbecue sauce. Slice the brisket against the grain of the meat, cutting thin slices. Stir the meat into the barbecue sauce and mix thoroughly. Add salt and pepper to taste.

Lay 1 sheet of filo on a large plastic cutting board. Brush some of the butter on the filo with a pastry brush. Layer a second and a third sheet of filo on top, brushing each one with butter. Put about 1½ cups of the brisket mixture in a long row across the narrow end of the filo. Roll up jelly roll fashion. Tuck the ends underneath. Place seam side down in a buttered pan. Repeat to form additional rolls until all the brisket has been used, placing each roll next to the previous one. Brush the tops and ends with melted butter.

Bake at 350° for 40 to 50 minutes, or until the filo is crisp and golden brown. Cut the rolls diagonally before serving. Serve hot.

SPINACH AND PROVOLONE POCKETS

◆

Makes 24 2-inch appetizers

¼ cup olive oil	1 teaspoon oregano
1 onion, chopped	1 teaspoon basil
4 garlic cloves, minced	1 pound filo leaves, thawed and
4 ounces pepperoni, sliced	covered with a damp kitchen
4 ounces mushrooms, sliced	towel
½ cup black olives, sliced	1 cup butter, clarified and melted
2 cups spinach, torn and stems	4 ounces provolone cheese, grated
removed	4 ounces mozzarella cheese, grated
salt and pepper	
2 egg yolks	
1 pound ricotta cheese	

◆

Butter a 9 × 13-inch pan; set aside. Preheat oven to 350°.

Heat the olive oil over medium heat in a large skillet. Cook the onion and garlic a couple of minutes, or until partially done (ingredients should still be firm). Drain well. Stir in the pepperoni, mushrooms, olives, and spinach. Add salt and pepper to taste and mix thoroughly. Set aside.

In a small bowl beat the egg yolks. Add the ricotta cheese, oregano, and basil and combine. Add salt and pepper to taste. Set aside.

Lay 1 sheet of filo on a large plastic cutting board. Brush some of the butter on the filo with a pastry brush. Layer a second and a third sheet of filo on top, brushing each one with butter. Put 1½ cups of the pepperoni mixture in a long row across the narrow end of the filo. Spread a thin layer of the ricotta mixture on the onions. Sprinkle ⅓ cup of both provolone and mozzarella cheese over the ricotta. Roll up jelly roll fashion. Tuck the ends underneath. Place the roll seam side down in the buttered pan. Repeat to form additional rolls until all of the filling has been used, placing each roll next to the previous one. Brush the tops and ends with the remaining melted butter.

Bake at 350° for 40 to 50 minutes, or until the filo is crisp and golden brown. Cut the rolls diagonally before serving. Serve hot.

TOMATO AND GREEN CHILI ROLL-UPS

◆

Makes 16 to 20

1½ pounds hamburger
1   onion, chopped
4   garlic cloves, minced
3   tomatoes, chopped
8   fresh green chilies (or 8 ounces canned, drained), chopped
    salt and pepper
4   egg yolks
1   pound sharp cheddar cheese, grated

    chili powder
1   pound filo leaves, thawed and covered with a damp kitchen towel
1   cup butter, clarified and melted

◆

Butter a 9 × 13-inch pan; set aside. Preheat oven to 350°.

Cook the hamburger, onion, and garlic over low heat in a large skillet until partially done (ingredients should be firm and meat should be slightly pink); drain well. Stir in the tomatoes and green chilies. Add salt and pepper to taste. Stir in the egg yolks and mix thoroughly. Set aside.

Lay 1 sheet of filo on a large plastic cutting board. Brush some of the butter on the filo with a pastry brush. Layer a second and a third sheet of filo on top, brushing each one with butter. Put 1½ cups of the hamburger mixture in a long row across the narrow end of the filo. Put about ¾ cup of the cheese along the center of the hamburger. Roll up jelly roll fashion. Tuck the ends underneath. Place the roll seam side down in the pan. Repeat to form additional rolls until all of the filling has been used, placing each roll next to the previous one. Brush the tops and ends with melted butter. Sprinkle the chili powder on top.

Bake at 350° for 40 to 50 minutes, or until the filo is crisp and golden brown. Cut the rolls diagonally before serving. Serve hot.

MUSHROOM-BACON BITES

◆

Makes 20 to 25

8	bacon slices		cayenne pepper
1	onion, chopped	½	pound filo leaves, thawed and
2	garlic cloves, minced		covered with a damp kitchen
1	pound mushrooms, thinly sliced		towel
½	cup fresh parsley, chopped	½	cup butter, clarified and melted
2	cups cracker crumbs		
	salt and pepper		

◆

Butter a 9 × 13-inch pan; set aside. Preheat oven to 350°.

Fry the bacon over medium-low heat in a medium skillet until done. Remove, drain, and set aside. Cook the onion in the drippings. Add the garlic and mushrooms to the onions and continue cooking until partially done (ingredients are still firm). Turn heat off and drain well. Stir in the parsley and cracker crumbs. Crumble the bacon and add to the mushroom mixture. Add the salt, pepper, and cayenne to taste. Set aside.

Lay several sheets of filo on a large plastic cutting board. Cut the sheets (lengthwise) into 2 sets of strips. Work with 1 strip at a time. Fold each strip lengthwise in thirds to form a long rectangle. Brush some of the butter on the filo with a pastry brush. Put 1 heaping tablespoon of the mushroom mixture in the center at one end of the rectangle. Fold the filo in thirds (lengthwise) again by folding the edges over the filling, encasing it, and roll jelly roll fashion. Place the little roll seam side down on the buttered pan. Repeat to form additional rolls until all the filling has been used, placing each little roll next to the previous one. Brush the tops and ends with the remaining melted butter.

Bake at 350° for 40 to 50 minutes, or until the filo is crisp and golden brown. Serve hot.

PIZZA ROLL-UPS

◆

Makes 16 to 20

1½ pounds bulk Italian sausage	15 ounces Italian tomato sauce
2 garlic cloves, minced	8 ounces tomato paste
1 bunch green onions, chopped	12 ounces mozzarella cheese, grated
2 green peppers, chopped	6 ounces Parmesan cheese, grated
2 tablespoons olive oil	5 ounces fontina cheese, grated
2 teaspoons Italian seasoning	1 pound filo leaves, thawed and
½ teaspoon crushed red pepper	covered with a damp kitchen
1 teaspoon salt	towel
¼ cup Chianti wine	1 cup butter, clarified and melted
2 teaspoons sugar	
4 ounces mushrooms, sliced	
5 ounces pepperoni, sliced	

◆

Butter a 9 × 13-inch pan; set aside. Preheat oven to 350°.

In a large skillet over low heat, cook the sausage, garlic, green onions, and green pepper in the olive oil until tender; drain well. Add the Italian seasoning, red pepper, salt, wine, sugar, mushrooms, and pepperoni. Stir until thoroughly combined. Stir in the tomato sauce and paste. Simmer on low heat for about 30 minutes, stirring often. Stir all of the grated cheeses into the sausage mixture. Thoroughly combine and set aside.

Lay 1 sheet of filo on a large plastic cutting board. Brush some of the butter on the filo with a pastry brush. Layer a second and a third sheet of filo on top, brushing each one with butter. Put 1½ cups of the sausage mixture in a long row across the narrow end of the filo. Roll up jelly roll fashion. Tuck the ends underneath. Place seam side down in the buttered pan. Repeat to form additional rolls until all of the sausage mixture has been used, placing each roll next to the previous one. Brush the tops and ends with melted butter.

Bake at 350° for 40 to 50 minutes, or until the filo is crisp and golden brown. Cut the rolls diagonally before serving. Serve hot.

BASIL-PINE NUT FINGERS

Makes 20 to 25

8 ounces cream cheese, at room temperature	½ pound filo leaves, thawed and covered with a damp kitchen towel
3 ounces Parmesan cheese, grated	½ cup butter, clarified and melted
½ cup fresh parsley, chopped	
1 teaspoon basil	
½ cup onion, chopped	
2 garlic cloves, minced	
2 egg yolks	
½ cup pine nuts (or almonds), chopped	
salt and pepper	
cayenne pepper	

◆

Butter a 9 × 13-inch pan; set aside. Preheat oven to 350°.

In a medium mixing bowl combine the cream cheese, Parmesan cheese, parsley, basil, onion, garlic, and egg yolks. Beat with an electric mixer until thoroughly mixed. Stir in the nuts. Add salt, pepper, and cayenne to taste. Set aside.

Lay several sheets of filo on a large plastic cutting board. Cut the sheets lengthwise into 2 sets of strips. Work with one strip at a time. Fold each strip in thirds lengthwise to form a long rectangle. Brush some of the butter on the filo with a pastry brush. Put 1 heaping tablespoon of the cheese mixture in the center of one end of the rectangle. Again fold the filo in thirds, lengthwise, by folding the edges over the filling, encasing it, and roll it in jelly roll fashion. Place the roll seam side down in the buttered pan. Repeat to form additional rolls until all of the filling has been used, placing each roll next to the previous one. Brush the tops and ends with the remaining melted butter. Sprinkle a little cayenne on top.

Bake at 350° for 40 to 50 minutes, or until the filo is crisp and golden brown. Serve hot.

SPANAKOPITA

◆

Makes 24

1 pound feta cheese, crumbled	salt and pepper
1 pound ricotta cheese	4 eggs, well beaten
4 ounces fresh Parmesan cheese, grated	1 pound filo leaves, thawed and covered with a damp kitchen towel
1 cup fresh parsley, finely chopped	
4 packages frozen spinach, thawed and well drained	1 cup butter, clarified and melted
1 large onion, chopped	

◆

Butter a 9 × 13-inch pan; set aside. Preheat oven to 350°.

In a large bowl, mix the feta, ricotta, and Parmesan cheeses. Stir in the parsley, spinach, and onion. Add salt and pepper to taste. Stir in the eggs and mix thoroughly.

Lay 1 sheet of filo on a large plastic cutting board. Brush some of the butter on the filo with a pastry brush. Layer a second and a third sheet of filo on top, brushing each one with butter. Put 1½ cups of filling in a long row across the narrow end of the filo. Roll up jelly roll fashion. Tuck the ends underneath. Place the roll seam side down in the buttered pan. Repeat to form additional rolls until all the filling has been used, placing each roll next to the previous one. Brush the tops and ends with the remaining melted butter.

Bake at 350° for 40 to 50 minutes, or until the filo is crisp and golden brown. Cut the rolls diagonally before serving. Serve hot.

CHILI RELLENO BAKE

Makes 20 to 24

1 onion, chopped	½ pound filo leaves, thawed and
4 garlic cloves, minced	covered with a damp kitchen
12 green chilies (or 12 ounces	towel
canned), seeded and chopped	½ cup butter, clarified and melted
¼ cup flour	12 ounces cheddar cheese, grated
1 cup milk	12 ounces Monterey Jack cheese,
4 eggs, well beaten	grated
salt and pepper	sour cream (optional)

◆

Butter a 9 × 13-inch pan; set aside. Preheat oven to 350°.

In a large bowl combine the onion, garlic, and green chilies. Set aside. In a medium bowl combine the flour and milk. Add the eggs and salt and pepper to taste. Mix thoroughly and set aside.

Place 1 sheet of filo in the bottom of the buttered pan, folding it to fit. Brush some of the butter on the filo with a pastry brush. Layer a second and a third sheet of filo on top, folding them to fit and brushing each one with butter. Spread the onion and green chili mixture evenly on the filo. Sprinkle the cheeses over the chili mixture. Pour the egg mixture over the cheese. Top with 3 or 4 sheets of folded, buttered filo. Before baking, sprinkle a few drops of water over the top and around the edges of the filo to prevent it from curling.

Bake at 350° for 40 to 50 minutes, or until the filo is crisp and golden brown. Serve hot with a tablespoon of sour cream on top of each serving, if desired.

LEEK PIE

◆

Makes 20 to 24

3	leeks	4	eggs, well beaten
1	quart boiling water, with 1 teaspoon salt added	¼	cup white wine
		1	pound ricotta cheese
½	cup margarine	½	pound feta cheese, crumbled
1	onion, chopped	1	cup fresh Parmesan cheese, grated
1	red onion, chopped		
1	bunch green onions, chopped		salt and pepper
2	garlic cloves, minced	1	pound filo leaves, thawed and covered with a damp kitchen towel
½	cup fresh parsley, chopped		
2	tablespoons fresh dill (or 2 teaspoons dried dill)		
1½	cups light cream	1	cup butter, clarified and melted
2	tablespoons cornstarch		sour cream (optional)

◆

Butter a 9 × 13-inch pan; set aside. Preheat oven to 350°.

Cut the stems off the leeks leaving 2 inches of stems beyond the bulbs. Wash several times in cold water. Cut into 1-inch rounds. Cook in the boiling water for 15 to 20 minutes and drain. After cooling a few minutes, chop into small pieces. Melt the margarine in a large skillet over medium heat, and sauté the leeks, all onions, and garlic until cooked but firm. Drain well. Stir in the parsley and dill and mix thoroughly. Set aside.

In a bowl, combine the cream and cornstarch. Add the well-beaten eggs and wine and mix thoroughly. Stir in the cheeses and mix thoroughly. Add salt and pepper to taste. Set aside.

Place 1 sheet of filo in the bottom of the buttered pan, folding it to fit. Brush some of the butter on the filo with a pastry brush. Layer a second and a third sheet of filo on top, folding them to fit and brushing each one with butter. Spread the leek and onion mixture evenly over the filo. Pour the egg and cheese mixture over the leeks. Layer 5 or 6 sheets of folded, buttered filo on top. Before baking, sprinkle a few drops of water over the top and around the edges of the filo to prevent it from curling.

Bake at 350° for 40 to 50 minutes, or until the filling is set and the filo is crisp and golden brown. Serve hot. Serve with sour cream, if desired.

GREEN CHILI AND CHEESE SQUARES

◆

Makes 24 2-inch appetizers

1	onion, chopped
1	bunch green onions, chopped
4	garlic cloves, minced
1	green pepper, chopped
1	red pepper, chopped
12	green chilies (or 10 ounces canned, drained) chopped
3	jalapeños, rinsed, seeded and chopped
3	tomatoes, chopped
½	cup black olives, chopped
1	cup milk
¼	cup cornstarch
5	eggs
	salt and pepper

½	pound filo leaves, thawed and covered with a damp kitchen towel
½	cup butter, clarified and melted
½	pound cheddar cheese, grated
½	pound longhorn cheese, grated
½	pound Monterey Jack cheese, grated
	sour cream (optional)

◆

Butter a 9 × 13-inch pan; set aside. Preheat oven to 350°.

Combine the onion, green onions, garlic, and peppers in a medium bowl and mix thoroughly. Stir in the green chilies, jalapeños, tomatoes, and olives. Mix thoroughly and set aside.

In another medium bowl combine the milk and cornstarch. Stir until the cornstarch dissolves. Add the eggs and beat thoroughly. Add salt and pepper to taste and mix thoroughly.

Place 1 sheet of filo in the bottom of the buttered pan, folding it to fit. Brush some of the butter on the filo with a pastry brush. Layer a second and a third sheet of filo on top, folding them to fit and brushing each one with butter. Spread the onion and chili mixture over the filo. Sprinkle all of the cheese over the onion and chili mixture. Pour the egg mixture over the cheese. Top with 3 or 4 sheets of folded, buttered filo. Before baking, sprinkle a few drops of water over the top and around the edges of the filo to prevent it from curling.

Bake at 350° for 40 to 50 minutes or until the filling is set and the filo is crisp and golden brown. Serve hot with a tablespoon of sour cream on top, if desired.

HAM AND SWISS BITES

Makes 20 to 25

2   egg yolks
8   ounces cream cheese, at room
        temperature
¼   cup sour cream
1   small onion, minced
2   teaspoons caraway seeds
4   ounces boiled ham, shredded
6   ounces Swiss cheese, grated

salt and pepper
½   pound filo leaves, thawed and
        covered with a damp kitchen
        towel
½   cup butter, clarified and melted

Butter a 9 × 13-inch pan; set aside. Preheat oven to 350°.

Beat the egg yolks in a medium mixing bowl with an electric mixer. Add the cream cheese, sour cream, onion, and caraway seeds and beat thoroughly. Stir in the ham and cheese. Add salt and pepper to taste. Set aside.

Lay several sheets of filo on a large plastic cutting board. Cut the sheets lengthwise into 2 sets of strips. Work with 1 strip at a time. Fold a strip in thirds lengthwise to form a long rectangle. Brush some of the butter on the filo with a pastry brush. Put 1 heaping tablespoon of the mixture in the center of one end of the rectangle. Again fold the filo in thirds lengthwise by folding the edges over the filling, encasing it, and roll the filo jelly roll fashion. Place the roll seam side down on the buttered pan. Repeat to form additional rolls until all the filling has been used, placing each roll next to the previous one. Brush the tops and ends with the remaining melted butter.

Bake at 350° for 40 to 50 minutes, or until the filo is crisp and golden brown. Serve hot or cold.

GARDEN VEGETABLE SQUARES

◆

Makes 20 to 24

4 eggs	1 large red or Vidalia onion, chopped
1½ pounds ricotta cheese	1 large green pepper, chopped
8 ounces cream cheese	1 cup mushrooms, sliced
2 envelopes (2 ounces) Italian or ranch-style salad dressing mix	1 cup broccoli florets
2 garlic cloves, minced	1 cup cauliflower florets
½ pound filo leaves, thawed and covered with a damp kitchen	½ cup fresh parsley, chopped salt and pepper
½ cup butter, clarified and melted	

◆

Butter a 9 × 13-inch pan; set aside. Preheat oven to 350°.

Beat eggs in a large mixing bowl with an electric mixer. Add the ricotta cheese and cream cheese and mix well. Add the dressing mix and garlic. Mix thoroughly and set aside.

Place 1 sheet of filo in the bottom of the buttered pan, folding it to fit. Brush some of the butter on the filo with a pastry brush. Layer a second and a third sheet of filo on top, folding them to fit and brushing each one with butter. Layer the onion, green pepper, mushrooms, broccoli, cauliflower, and parsley over the filo. Add salt and pepper to taste. Pour the cheese mixture over the vegetables. Top with 2 or 3 sheets of folded, buttered filo. Before baking, sprinkle a few drops of water over the top and around the edges of the filo to prevent it from curling.

Bake at 350° for 40 to 50 minutes, or until cheese is set and filo is crisp and golden brown. Serve hot or cold.

FETA PUFFS

Makes 10 to 12

1 onion, chopped	5 eggs, well beaten
½ cup green onions, chopped	1 pound filo leaves, thawed and
1 pound feta cheese, crumbled	covered with a damp kitchen
1 pound ricotta cheese	towel
8 ounces cream cheese, at room temperature	1 cup butter, clarified and melted
½ cup fresh parsley, chopped salt and pepper	

Butter a 7 × 11-inch pan; set aside. Preheat oven to 350°.

Combine the onion, green onions, feta, ricotta, and cream cheese in a large bowl. Beat with an electric mixer until creamy. Stir in the parsley and add the salt and pepper to taste. Stir in the eggs and thoroughly combine.

Place 1 sheet of filo in the bottom of the buttered pan, folding to fit. Brush some of the butter on the filo with a pastry brush. Layer a second and a third sheet of filo on top, folding them to fit and brushing each one with butter. Spread the mixture on the filo. Top with 2 or 3 sheets of folded, buttered filo. Before baking, sprinkle a few drops of water over the top and around the edges of the filo to prevent it from curling.

Bake at 350° for 40 to 50 minutes, or until the filo is crisp and golden brown. Serve hot.

EXTRAORDINARY ENTREES

GRUYERE TART

Serves 6

2   cups cream (or light cream)
¼   cup cornstarch
5   eggs, well beaten
½   pound sharp cheddar cheese, grated
⅓   pound Gruyere cheese, grated
¼   pound smoked cheese, grated

salt and pepper
cayenne pepper
½   pound filo leaves, thawed and covered with a damp kitchen towel
½   cup butter, clarified and melted

Butter a 6 × 10-inch pan; set aside. Preheat oven to 350°.

In a double boiler, combine the cream and cornstarch. Stir until the cornstarch dissolves. Cook over—not immersed in—boiling water. Stir the well-beaten eggs into the cream mixture. Continue stirring until smooth and slightly thickened. Stir in the cheeses. Add salt, pepper, and cayenne to taste. Remove from heat and set aside.

Place 1 sheet of filo in the bottom of the buttered pan, folding it to fit. Brush some of the butter on the filo with a pastry brush. Layer 2 or 3 sheets of folded, buttered filo. Pour the cheese filling on the filo. Top with 2 or 3 folded, buttered sheets of filo. Sprinkle a little cayenne on top. Before baking, sprinkle a few drops of water over the top and around the edges of the filo to prevent it from curling.

Bake at 350° for 40 to 50 minutes, or until the filling is set and the filo is golden brown and crisp. Serve hot.

FILO-WRAPPED CHICKEN AND SMOKED SAUSAGE GUMBO

Serves 5 to 6

4   slices bacon, cut into 2-inch strips
1   pound smoked sausage, cut into 1-inch pieces
4   chicken breast halves, boned, skinned, and cut in 2-inch wide strips
1   cup green onions, chopped
1   onion, chopped
2   garlic cloves, minced
1   green pepper, chopped
1   cup celery, chopped
2   cups okra (fresh, frozen, or canned) chopped

¼   cup flour
2   cups chicken stock (or bouillon)
½   cups fresh parsley, chopped
    salt and pepper
    cayenne pepper
2   cups bread crumbs (or croutons), buttered and toasted*
1   pound filo leaves, thawed and covered with a damp kitchen towel
1   cup butter, clarified and melted

Butter a 9 × 13-inch pan; set aside. Preheat oven to 350°.

Fry the bacon in a large skillet over medium-low heat, until crisp. Remove bacon and place on paper towels to drain. Put the sausage and chicken into the skillet and cook, over low heat, in the drippings until the chicken is partially done, or slightly pink. Remove to paper towels and drain. Over low heat, cook the green onions, onion, garlic, green pepper, celery, and okra in the remaining drippings until partially done (ingredients should still be firm). Remove with slotted spoon, drain, and set aside. Stir the flour into the drippings, continue stirring until it is thick and pastelike. Stir in the chicken stock and thoroughly mix. Cook while stirring, over low heat, until the stock is smooth and thickened. Stir in the parsley, bacon, sausage, and chicken. Add the green onions, onions, garlic, peppers, celery, and okra. Add the salt, pepper and cayenne to taste. Turn the heat off and set aside.

Place 1 sheet of filo in the bottom of the buttered pan, folding it to fit. Brush some of the butter on the filo with a pastry brush. Layer a second and a third sheet of folded, buttered filo on top. Put half of the bread crumbs (or rice) on the filo, spreading it evenly. Spoon half of the sausage and chicken mixture over the bread crumbs. Layer 2 or 3 more layers of filo on top of the filling. Sprinkle the remaining

*2 cups cooked rice may be substituted for the bread crumbs.

bread crumbs over the filo and top with the rest of the meat filling. Cover with 4 or 5 folded, buttered sheets of filo. Before baking, sprinkle a few drops of water over the top and around the edges of the filo to prevent it from curling.

Bake at 350° for 40 to 50 minutes, or until the filo is crisp and golden brown. Serve hot.

MEDITERRANEAN CASSEROLE

◆

Serves 6

2 cups cream (or light cream)	½ cup black olives, sliced
2 tablespoons cornstarch	salt and pepper
2 tablespoons butter	6 ounces mozzarella cheese, grated
2 cups onion, chopped	2 ounces Parmesan cheese, grated
2 garlic cloves, minced	½ pound filo leaves, thawed and
3 tablespoons fresh basil (or 1	covered with a damp kitchen
tablespoon dried), chopped	towel
1 teaspoon dry mustard	½ cup butter, clarified and melted
1 tablespoon sugar	1 tomato, chopped
6 egg yolks	salt and pepper

◆

Butter a 6 × 10-inch pan; set aside. Preheat oven to 350°.

In a double boiler, combine the cream and cornstarch. Stir until the cornstarch dissolves. Stir in the butter, onion, garlic, basil, mustard, and sugar. Cook over—not immersed in—boiling water. Continue stirring until the butter melts. In a mixing bowl, beat egg yolks thoroughly; stir in 2 tablespoons of the hot mixture and mix thoroughly. Stir the yolk mixture into the heated custard. Continue stirring until smooth and partially thickened. Add the olives and salt and pepper to taste. Stir in the cheeses and mix thoroughly. Remove from heat and set aside.

Place 1 sheet of filo in the bottom of the buttered pan, folding it to fit. Brush some of the butter on the filo with a pastry brush. Layer a second and a third sheet of filo on top, folding them to fit the pan and brushing each one with butter. Sprinkle the tomato over the filo. Salt and pepper the tomato. Pour the custard over the tomato. Top with 2 or 3 folded, buttered sheets of filo. Before baking, sprinkle a few drops of water over the top and around the edges of the filo to prevent it from curling.

Bake at 350° for 40 to 50 minutes, or until the custard is set and the filo is golden and crisp. Serve hot.

CRAB NEWBURG

◆

Serves 5 to 6

Wine Sauce
¼   cup butter
1   tablespoon flour (or cornstarch)
1½ cups cream (or light cream)
3   egg yolks, well beaten
¼   cup Madeira (or sherry)
    salt and pepper

¼   cup margarine
¼   cup onion, chopped
½   pound mushrooms, sliced
½   cup green pepper, chopped

1   pound crab meat (fresh, frozen, or canned)
½   cup fresh parsley, chopped
    salt and pepper
    cayenne pepper
½   pound filo leaves, thawed and covered with a damp kitchen towel
½   cup butter, clarified and melted
2   cups bread crumbs, toasted
1   cup Parmesan cheese, grated

◆

Butter a 9 × 13-inch pan; set aside. Preheat oven to 350°.

Wine Sauce
Melt butter in a small saucepan over low heat. Add the flour and stir until it forms a paste. Stir in the cream and well-beaten egg yolks. Stir in the Madeira. Add salt and pepper to taste. Stir until smooth and slightly thickened. Set aside.

Melt the margarine over low heat in a medium skillet. Cook the onion, mushrooms, green pepper, and crab until partially done (ingredients should still be firm). Drain well. Stir in the parsley and mix thoroughly. Add salt, pepper, and cayenne to taste. Set aside.

Lay 1 sheet of filo on a large plastic cutting board. Brush some of the butter on the filo with a pastry brush. Layer a second and a third sheet of filo on top, brushing each one with butter. Sprinkle about ⅓ cup of the bread crumbs over the filo. Put 1½ cups of the crab mixture in a long row, across the narrow end of the filo. Put about 2 tablespoons of Parmesan cheese on the crab. Put about 2 tablespoons of the sauce on the cheese. Roll up jelly roll fashion. Tuck the ends underneath. Place seam side down in the buttered pan. Repeat to form additional rolls until all the crab mixture has been used, placing each roll next to the previous one. Brush the tops and ends with melted butter.

Bake at 350° for 40 to 50 minutes, or until the filo is crisp and golden brown. Cut the rolls diagonally before serving. Serve hot with the Wine Sauce.

❖❖❖

FILO LASAGNA

◆

Serves 12

1	pound bulk Italian sausage		salt and pepper
1	pound hamburger		crushed red pepper
1	onion, chopped	1	pound ricotta cheese
3	garlic cloves, minced	12	ounces mozzarella cheese, grated
½	pound mushrooms, thinly sliced	6	ounces Romano cheese, grated
15	ounces Italian-style tomato sauce	1	pound filo leaves, thawed and
15	ounces tomato paste		covered with a damp
6	ounces consomme (or beef stock)		kitchen towel
14	ounces Italian-style stewed	1	cup butter, clarified and melted
	tomatoes		
½	cup red wine		
2	teaspoons basil		
2	teaspoons oregano		
1	tablespoon sugar		

◆

Butter a 9 × 13-inch pan; set aside. Preheat oven to 350°.

In a large skillet or Dutch oven combine the sausage and hamburger and cook over medium-low heat, stirring often. Add the onion and garlic and cook until the sausage and hamburger are partially done (meat should be slightly pink). Drain well. Stir in the mushrooms, tomato sauce, tomato paste, consomme, stewed tomatoes, and wine. Stir thoroughly. Add the basil, oregano, and sugar. Add salt, pepper, and crushed red pepper to taste. Simmer over low heat for an hour, stirring frequently. Set aside.

Place 1 sheet of filo in the bottom of the buttered pan, folding it to fit. Brush some of the butter on the filo with a pastry brush. Layer a second and a third sheet of filo on top, folding them to fit and brushing each one with butter. Put half of the meat mixture on the buttered filo, spreading it evenly. Layer half of the ricotta, mozzarella, and Romano cheese over the meat. Lay 3 more buttered sheets of filo over the cheese. Top with the rest of the meat and cheese. Cover with 6 or 7 sheets of folded, buttered filo. Before baking, sprinkle a few drops of water over the top and around the edges of the filo to prevent it from curling.

Bake at 350° about 1 hour, or until the filo is crisp and golden brown. Serve hot.

Note: If lasagna is to be served on another day, cover well and freeze. Thaw at room temperature for a few hours. Reheat at 350° for 30 to 45 minutes.

CHICKEN SALAD ROLLS

◆

Serves 6

½   cup margarine
4   chicken breast halves, skinned, boned and cubed
½   cup green onions, chopped
½   cup green pepper, chopped
½   cup celery, chopped
¾   cup almonds (or walnuts or pecans), chopped
½   cup fresh parsley, chopped
½   cup crushed pineapple, drained
⅓   cup pickle relish

3   hard-boiled eggs, chopped
    salt and pepper
1   tablespoon sugar
2   tablespoons white vinegar
2   tablespoons amaretto
1   cup sour cream
½   pound filo leaves, thawed and covered with a damp kitchen towel
½   cup butter, clarified and melted

◆

Butter a 7 × 11-inch pan; set aside. Preheat oven to 350°.

Melt the margarine over low heat in a large skillet. Cook the chicken a few minutes until partially done (meat should be slightly pink). Remove and set aside. Cook the onion, green pepper, and celery a couple of minutes, until partially done (ingredients should still be firm). Drain well. Add the chicken, almonds, parsley, pineapple, pickle relish and chopped eggs. Add salt and pepper to taste. Mix thoroughly and set aside.

In a small dish combine the sugar, vinegar, amaretto, and sour cream. Stir this into the chicken mixture and mix thoroughly. Set aside.

Lay 1 sheet of filo on a large plastic cutting board. Fold it in half, lengthwise, to form a rectangle. Brush some of the butter on the filo with a pastry brush. Center about 1 cup of the chicken salad at one end of the filo. Roll up jelly roll fashion. Tuck the ends underneath. Place the roll in the buttered dish seam side down. Repeat to form additional rolls until all the chicken filling has been used, placing each roll next to the previous one. Brush completely with butter.

Bake at 350° for 40 to 50 minutes, or until the filo is crisp and golden brown. Serve hot.

❖❖❖

CHICKEN DIVAN

◆

Serves 5 or 6

4	chicken breast halves, boned, skinned, cut into strips		salt and pepper
½	cup butter (or margarine)	1	bunch broccoli florets
¼	pound mushrooms, sliced	½	pound filo leaves, thawed and covered with a damp kitchen towel
1	tablespoon flour		
1	cup chicken stock (or bouillon)	½	cup butter, clarified and melted
1	cup sour cream	4	ounces Parmesan cheese, grated
¼	cup white wine	4	ounces Monterey Jack cheese, grated
1	tablespoon lemon juice		
2	teaspoons curry powder		
1	teaspoon basil		

◆

Butter a 7 × 11-inch pan; set aside. Preheat oven to 350°.

Melt the butter in a large skillet over low heat. Cook the chicken until partially done, or still slightly pink. Remove chicken and set aside. Add the mushrooms to the skillet and cook a couple of minutes, until partially done (mushrooms should still be firm). Remove and set aside. Stir the flour into the drippings and mix thoroughly. Add the chicken stock and continue stirring over low heat. Blend in the sour cream. Stir in the wine, lemon juice, curry powder, and basil. Add salt and pepper to taste and mix thoroughly, stirring until the sauce is smooth and slightly thickened. Turn the heat off and stir in the chicken, mushrooms, and broccoli. Set aside.

Place 1 sheet of filo in the bottom of the buttered pan, folding it to fit. Brush some of the butter on the filo with a pastry brush. Layer a second and a third sheet of filo on top, folding them to fit and brushing each one with butter. Spread the chicken mixture on the filo. Sprinkle the cheeses over the chicken. Top with 2 or 3 sheets of folded, buttered filo. Before baking, sprinkle a few drops of water over the top and around the edges of the filo to prevent it from curling.

Bake at 350° for 40 to 50 minutes, or until the filo is crisp and golden brown. Serve hot.

PORK TENDERLOIN STRUDEL
WITH WINE SAUCE

Serves 4

5 slices bacon	***Wine Sauce***
½ pound pork tenderloin, thinly sliced	2 tablespoons butter
1 onion, chopped	1 tablespoon flour (or cornstarch)
¾ pound mushrooms, sliced	½ cup cream (or light cream)
½ cup pepperoni, sliced	¼ cup red (or rosé) wine
½ cup fresh parsley, chopped	½ cup beef stock (or bouillon)
2 cups bread crumbs	1 tablespoon Worcestershire sauce
2 teaspoons basil	2 tablespoons honey
salt and pepper	salt and pepper
½ pound filo leaves, thawed and covered with a damp kitchen towel	
½ cup butter, clarified and melted	

Butter a 7 × 11-inch pan; set aside. Preheat oven to 350°.

Cook the bacon over medium-low heat in a large skillet. Remove bacon, drain, and set aside. Cook the tenderloin, onion, and mushrooms in the drippings, cooking the meat just until partially done (meat should be slightly pink). Drain the skillet. Stir in the pepperoni, parsley, bread crumbs and basil. Add salt and pepper to taste. Crumble the bacon and add it to the stuffing in the skillet. Mix thoroughly and set aside.

Lay 1 sheet of filo on a large plastic cutting board and fold it in half (lengthwise) to form a rectangle. Brush some of the butter on the filo with a pastry brush. Center a couple of slices of pork at one end of the filo. Put ½ cup of the stuffing on top of the pork. Roll up jelly roll fashion. Tuck the ends underneath. Place the roll in the buttered dish seam side down. Repeat to form additional rolls until all the pork has been used, placing each roll next to the previous one. Brush completely with butter.

Bake at 350° for 40 to 50 minutes, or until the filo is crisp and golden brown. Serve hot with the Wine Sauce.

Wine Sauce

Melt the butter over low heat in a saucepan. Add the flour and stir until a thick paste forms. Stir in the cream, wine, and beef stock. Continue stirring until smooth and slightly thickened. Stir in the Worcestershire sauce, honey, and add salt and pepper to taste.

SPINACH- AND WALNUT-STUFFED FILO

◆

Serves 5 to 8

½	cup butter (or margarine)	½	pound fresh spinach, washed, drained, chopped, and stems discarded
1	large onion, chopped		
½	pound mushrooms, sliced		
2	tablespoons cornstarch	1	cup walnuts, chopped
1	cup sour cream		salt and pepper
3	eggs, well beaten	½	pound filo leaves, thawed and covered with a damp kitchen towel
2	tablespoons sherry		
2	teaspoons dill		
½	cup fresh parsley, chopped	½	cup butter, clarified and melted

◆

Butter a 7 × 11-inch pan; set aside. Preheat oven to 350°.

Melt the butter in a medium skillet over low heat. Cook the onion and mushrooms until partially done but still firm. Remove with a slotted spoon and set aside. Stir the cornstarch into the drippings in the skillet and stir until a paste forms. Stir in the sour cream and continue stirring until smooth. Add the well-beaten eggs, sherry, dill, and parsley and mix thoroughly. Stir in the spinach, walnuts, onions, and mushrooms. Add the salt and pepper to taste and mix thoroughly.

Place 1 sheet of filo in the bottom of the buttered pan, folding it to fit. Brush some of the butter on the filo with a pastry brush. Layer a second and a third sheet of folded, buttered filo on top. Put the filling on the filo, spreading it evenly. Layer 2 or 3 sheets of folded, buttered filo over the spinach mixture. Before baking, sprinkle a few drops of water over the top and around the edges of the filo to prevent it from curling.

Bake at 350° for 40 to 50 minutes, or until the filo is crisp and golden brown. Serve hot.

CHICKEN KIEV WITH SHERRY SAUCE

Serves 4

½ cup butter, melted
¼ cup fresh parsley, chopped
1 tablespoon chives
1 garlic clove, minced
½ teaspoon salt
⅛ teaspoon pepper
4 chicken breast halves, skinned
     and boned
½ pound filo leaves, thawed and
     covered with a damp
     kitchen towel
½ cup butter, clarified and melted

2 ounces mozzarella cheese, grated

Sherry Sauce
4 tablespoons butter, divided
¼ pound mushrooms, sliced
1 tablespoon flour (or cornstarch)
½ cup cream (or light cream)
¼ cup sherry
½ cup chicken stock (or bouillon)
   salt and pepper

Butter a 9 × 13-inch pan; set aside. Preheat oven to 350°.

Combine the melted butter, parsley, chives, garlic, salt, and pepper in a small dish. Freeze until firm.

Place each chicken breast between 2 pieces of plastic wrap. Pound with a mallet until ¼ inch thick. Set aside. Cut the frozen butter into 4 pieces and place 1 piece on each chicken breast.

Lay 1 sheet filo on a large plastic cutting board and fold it in half, lengthwise, to form a rectangle. Brush some of the butter on the filo with a pastry brush. Center a chicken breast at one end of the filo. Put ¼ cup of cheese on top of the butter. Roll up jelly roll fashion. Tuck the ends underneath. Place the roll in the buttered dish seam side down. Repeat to form 3 more rolls, placing each roll next to the previous one. Brush completely with butter.

Bake at 350° for 40 to 50 minutes, or until the filo is crisp and golden brown. Serve hot with the hot Sherry Sauce.

Sherry Sauce
Melt 2 tablespoons butter over low heat in a small skillet. Cook the mushrooms until done. Drain well and set aside. Melt the rest of the butter over low heat in a saucepan, add the flour and stir until a paste forms. Stir in the cream, sherry, and chicken stock. Stir until smooth and slightly thickened. Add the mushrooms. Add salt and pepper to taste.

LOBSTER NEWBURG

◆

Serves 4

Wine Sauce
¼ cup butter
2 tablespoons cornstarch
1½ cups cream (or light cream)
4 egg yolks, well beaten
¼ cup Madeira
2 teaspoons lemon juice
2 teaspoons nutmeg
¼ teaspoon paprika
salt and pepper

¼ cup butter
½ pound mushrooms, sliced

4 1½ pound lobsters, cooked,
   cleaned, and cubed
   salt
   white pepper
   cayenne pepper
½ pound filo leaves, thawed and
   covered with a damp
   kitchen towel
½ cup butter, clarified and melted
2 cups bread crumbs, toasted

◆

Butter a 7 × 11-inch pan; set aside. Preheat oven to 350°.

Wine Sauce
Melt butter in a saucepan over low heat. Add the cornstarch and stir until it forms a paste. Stir in the cream and well-beaten egg yolks and continue stirring until well blended. Stir in the Madeira, lemon juice, nutmeg and paprika. Add salt and pepper to taste. Stir until sauce is smooth and slightly thickened. Set aside.

Melt butter in a medium skillet over low heat. Cook the mushrooms until partially done (they should still be firm); drain well. Stir in the lobster and mix thoroughly. Add salt, pepper, and cayenne to taste. Set aside.

Lay 1 sheet of filo on a large plastic cutting board. Brush some of the butter on the filo with a pastry brush. Layer a second and a third sheet of filo on top, brushing each with butter. Sprinkle about ⅓ cup of the bread crumbs over the filo. Put 1½ cups of the lobster mixture in a long row across narrow end of the filo. Put about ½ cup of the sauce on the lobster. Roll up jelly roll fashion. Tuck the ends underneath. Place seam side down in the buttered pan. Repeat to form additional rolls until all of the lobster has been used, placing each roll next to the previous one. Brush the tops and ends with melted butter.

Bake at 350° for 40 to 50 minutes, or until the filo is crisp and golden brown. Cut the rolls diagonally before serving. Serve hot with remaining sauce.

GREEN PEPPER AND CHICKEN WITH
BLUE CHEESE SAUCE

Serves 5 to 6

Blue Cheese Sauce
¼ cup butter
2 tablespoons flour (or cornstarch)
½ cup cream (or light cream)
½ cup chicken stock (or bouillon)
¼ cup white wine
6 ounces blue cheese, crumbled
   salt and pepper

¼ cup margarine
1 bunch green onions, chopped
½ pound mushrooms, washed and
   sliced

½ cup green pepper, chopped
6 chicken breast halves, skinned,
   boned and cut into strips
½ cup fresh parsley, chopped
   salt and pepper
½ pound filo leaves, thawed and
   covered with a damp
   kitchen towel
½ cup butter, clarified and melted
2 cups bread crumbs, toasted

Blue Cheese Sauce

Melt the butter in a saucepan over low heat. Add the flour and stir until a paste forms. Stir in the cream and chicken stock. Stir in the wine and blue cheese. Add salt and pepper to taste. Stir until the cheese melts and mixture is smooth and slightly thickened. Set aside.

Butter a 9 × 13-inch pan; set aside. Preheat oven to 350°.

Melt the margarine in a medium skillet over low heat. Cook the onions, mushrooms, green pepper, and chicken until partially done (vegetables should be firm and meat should be slightly pink). Drain well. Stir in the parsley and add salt and pepper to taste and mix thoroughly. Set aside.

Lay 1 sheet of filo on a large plastic cutting board. Brush some of the butter on the filo with a pastry brush. Layer a second and a third sheet of filo on top, brushing each with butter. Sprinkle about ⅓ cup of the bread crumbs over the filo. Put 1½ cups of the chicken filling in a long row across narrow end of the filo. Put about ¼ cup of the sauce on the chicken. Roll up jelly roll fashion. Tuck the ends underneath. Place seam side down in the buttered pan. Repeat to form additional rolls until all of the chicken has been used, placing each roll next to the previous one. Brush the tops and ends with melted butter.

Bake at 350° for 40 to 50 minutes, or until the filo is crisp and golden brown. Cut the rolls diagonally before serving. Serve hot with the Blue Cheese Sauce.

MUENSTER CHEESE AND TURKEY STRUDEL WITH MADEIRA SAUCE

◆

Serves 10 to 12

1	small turkey (about 2 pounds) cooked, skinned, and boned	1	pound filo leaves, thawed and covered with a damp kitchen towel
1	onion, chopped	1	cup butter, clarified and melted
1	pound mushrooms, sliced		
½	cup margarine		***Madeira Sauce***
1	pound Muenster cheese, grated	¼	cup butter
4	ounces fresh Romano cheese, grated	2	tablespoons flour (or cornstarch)
		1	cup cream (or light cream)
½	cup fresh parsley, chopped	¼	cup Madeira wine
	salt and pepper	1	cup chicken stock (or bouillon)
2	cups bread crumbs, toasted		salt and pepper

◆

Butter a 9 × 13-inch pan; set aside. Preheat oven to 350°.

Cube the turkey and put it in a large mixing bowl. In a medium skillet, cook the onion and mushrooms in the margarine over low heat. Drain well. Mix the onion and mushrooms with the turkey.

Add the Muenster and Romano cheese to the turkey mixture. Stir in the parsley. Add salt and pepper to taste and mix thoroughly.

Lay 1 sheet of filo on a large plastic cutting board. Brush some of the butter on the filo with a pastry brush. Layer a second and a third sheet of filo on top, brushing each one with butter. Sprinkle about ⅓ cup of the bread crumbs over the filo. Put 1½ cups of the turkey mixture in a long row across narrow end of the filo. Roll up jelly roll fashion. Tuck the ends underneath. Place the roll seam side down in the buttered pan. Repeat to form additional rolls until all the turkey filling has been used, placing each roll next to the previous one. Brush the tops and ends with melted butter.

Bake at 350° for 40 to 50 minutes, or until the filo is crisp and golden brown. Cut the rolls diagonally before serving. Serve hot with the Madeira Sauce.

Madeira Sauce
Melt the butter over low heat in a small saucepan. Add the flour and stir until a paste forms. Stir in the cream, Madeira, and chicken stock. Continue stirring until smooth and slightly thickened. Add salt and pepper to taste.

ALMOND-CHICKEN STRUDEL
WITH AMARETTO SAUCE

◆

Serves 4

¼   cup margarine
½   cup onion, chopped
¾   pound mushrooms, sliced
¾   cup almonds, chopped or slivered
½   cup fresh parsley, chopped
1   tablespoon chives
    salt and pepper
4   chicken breast halves, skinned
        and boned
½   pound filo leaves, thawed and
        covered with a damp
        kitchen towel
½   cup butter, clarified and melted

Amaretto Sauce
2   tablespoons butter
1   tablespoon flour (or cornstarch)
½   cup cream (or light cream)
¼   cup amaretto
½   cup chicken stock (or bouillon)
    salt and pepper

◆

Butter a 7 × 11-inch pan; set aside. Preheat oven to 350°.

Melt the margarine in a small skillet over low heat. Cook the onion and
mushrooms, until partially done and still firm. Drain well. Stir in the almonds,
parsley, and chives. Add salt and pepper to taste. Set aside.

Place each chicken breast between 2 pieces of plastic wrap. Pound with a mallet
until ¼ inch thick. Set aside.

Lay 1 sheet of filo on a large plastic cutting board and fold it in half, lengthwise, to
form a rectangle. Brush some of the butter on the filo with a pastry brush.
Center a chicken breast half at one end of the filo. Put ½ cup of mushroom mixture
on top of the chicken breast. Roll up jelly roll fashion. Tuck the ends
underneath. Place the roll in the buttered dish seam side down. Repeat to form 3
more rolls, placing each roll next to the previous one. Brush completely with
butter.

Bake at 350° for 40 to 50 minutes, or until the filo is crisp and golden brown. Make
the sauce while the chicken is cooking.

Amaretto Sauce

Melt the butter in a saucepan over low heat. Add the flour and stir until a thick paste forms. Stir in the cream, amaretto, and chicken stock. Continue stirring until smooth and slightly thickened. Add salt and pepper to taste. Serve hot over the hot strudel.

SPINACH TART

Makes 9 to 12 3-inch servings

16 ounces cream cheese, at room temperature	¾ cup almonds, sliced or chopped, divided
1 cup sour cream	1 pound Swiss cheese, grated
1 bunch green onions, chopped	½ pound filo leaves, thawed and covered with a damp kitchen towel
2 packages vegetable soup mix	
10 ounces frozen spinach, thawed and well drained	½ cup butter, clarified and melted
4 eggs, well beaten	

◆

Butter a 9 × 13-inch pan; set aside. Preheat oven to 350°

In a large bowl combine the cream cheese, sour cream, green onions, and soup mix. Beat thoroughly with a mixer. Add the spinach and mix thoroughly. Stir in the well-beaten eggs and ½ cup almonds. Stir in the cheese and blend well. Set aside.

Place 1 sheet of filo in the bottom of the buttered pan, folding it to fit. Brush some of the butter on the filo with a pastry brush. Layer 2 or 3 sheets of folded, buttered filo on top. Put the spinach mixture on the filo, spreading it out evenly. Top with 4 or 5 sheets of folded, buttered filo. Sprinkle the remaining almonds on top. Before baking, sprinkle a few drops of water over the top and around the edges of the filo to prevent it from curling.

Bake at 350° for 40 to 50 minutes, or until the filo is golden brown and crisp. Serve hot.

CHINESE CHICKEN AND VEGETABLE STRUDEL WITH PLUM SAUCE

◆

Makes 10 to 12 3-inch servings

½ cup margarine
1 onion, chopped
1 green pepper, chopped
1 stalk celery, chopped
3 chicken breast halves, skinned, boned, sliced into strips
½ pound mushrooms, sliced
1 cup broccoli florets
1 cup cauliflower florets
¼ pound snow peas
½ small head cabbage, shredded
6 ounces pineapple tidbits, well drained
6 ounces water chestnuts, sliced
½ cup almonds, sliced
  soy sauce
  black pepper

1 pound filo leaves, thawed and covered with a damp kitchen towel
1 cup butter, clarified and melted
¼ cup almonds, sliced

Plum sauce
12 ounces plum jam
⅓ cup chili sauce
1 tablespoon lemon juice
1½ teaspoons garlic powder
  soy sauce

◆

Butter a 9 × 13-inch pan; set aside. Preheat oven to 350°.

Melt the margarine in a large skillet over medium heat. Add the onion, green pepper, celery, chicken, and mushrooms and cook until the vegetables are still firm and chicken is slightly pink. Drain well. Remove from heat and stir in the broccoli, cauliflower, snow peas, cabbage, pineapple, water chestnuts, and almonds; mix thoroughly. Add the soy sauce and pepper to taste.

Lay 1 sheet of filo on a large plastic cutting board. Brush some of the butter on the filo with a pastry brush. Layer a second and a third sheet of filo on top, brushing each with butter. Put 1½ cups of the chicken filling in a long row at the narrow end of the filo. Roll up jelly roll fashion. Tuck the ends underneath. Place the roll seam side down in the buttered pan. Repeat to form additional rolls until all of the filling has been used, placing each roll next to the previous one. Brush rolls with the remaining melted butter. Sprinkle the almonds on top.

Bake at 350° for 40 to 50 minutes, or until the filo is crisp and golden brown. Cut the rolls diagonally before serving. Serve hot with plum sauce and soy sauce.

Plum Sauce

In a medium bowl, combine the plum jam, chili sauce, lemon juice, and garlic powder. Stir until smooth. Serve plum sauce at room temperature. Refrigerate remaining sauce.

CANADIAN BACON AND SWISS CHEESE STRUDEL

◆

Serves 6 to 8

½	onion, chopped	½	pound filo leaves, thawed and
4	ounces canned, sliced		covered with a damp
	mushrooms		kitchen towel
½	cup black olives, sliced	½	cup butter, clarified and melted
4	ounces Swiss cheese, grated	1	pound Canadian bacon, thinly
4	ounces Muenster cheese, grated		sliced
2	egg yolks, well beaten		

◆

Butter a 7 × 11-inch pan; set aside. Preheat oven to 350°.

In a medium bowl combine the onion, mushrooms, and olives. Stir in the Swiss and Muenster cheese, mixing completely. Stir in the egg yolks and mix well. Set aside.

Lay 1 sheet of filo on a large plastic cutting board. Brush some of the butter on the filo with a pastry brush. Layer a second and a third sheet of filo on top, brushing each with butter. Lay the sliced bacon in a long row across the narrow end of the filo. Spoon some of the cheese mixture (about ¾ cup) on top of the bacon. Roll up jelly roll fashion. Tuck the ends underneath. Place the roll seam side down in the buttered pan. Repeat to form additional rolls until all the bacon and cheese have been used, placing each roll next to the previous one. Brush the tops with the melted butter.

Bake at 350° for 40 to 50 minutes, or until the filo is crisp and golden brown. Slice the rolls diagonally before serving. Serve hot.

Note: This dish is quick and easy to make when you are short on time.

SCALLOP STRUDEL
WITH WINE SAUCE

◆

Serves 8 to 10

1½ pounds fresh scallops or (frozen
     scallops, thawed)
½   cup flour
1   teaspoon salt, divided
1   teaspoon pepper, divided
½   cup of vegetable oil
½   cup butter (or margarine)
1   bunch green onions, chopped
¾   pound mushrooms, sliced
12 ounces Swiss cheese, grated
16 ounces cream cheese, at room
     temperature
2   tablespoons fresh parsley,
     chopped
2   cups bread crumbs, toasted,
     divided

1   pound filo leaves, thawed and
     covered with a damp
     kitchen towel
1   cup butter, clarified and melted

Wine Sauce

¼   cup butter
2   tablespoons flour (or cornstarch)
1   cup cream (or light cream)
¼   cup white wine
1   cup chicken stock (or bouillon)
    salt and pepper

◆

Butter a 9 × 13-inch pan; set aside. Preheat oven to 350°.

If the scallops are very large, cut into 1½-inch pieces, drain, and pat dry. Mix the
flour, ½ teaspoon of salt and a dash of pepper in a small bowl. Coat the
scallops in the flour mixture. Heat the oil over medium-low heat, in a medium
skillet and add the scallops. Cook the scallops, turning them carefully, until
light brown, about 5 minutes. Drain well and put in a large bowl.

Melt the butter over low heat in the skillet, and cook the green onions and
mushrooms until partially done or still firm. Drain well. Stir the green onions
and mushrooms into the scallops. Add the Swiss cheese and cream cheese and
mix thoroughly. Stir in the parsley and add salt and pepper to taste.

Lay 1 sheet of filo on a large plastic cutting board. Brush some of the butter on the
filo with a pastry brush. Layer a second and a third sheet of filo on top,
brushing each with butter. Sprinkle about ½ cup of the bread crumbs over the
buttered filo. Put 1½ cups of the scallop mixture in a long row across the
narrow end of the filo. Roll up jelly roll fashion. Tuck the ends underneath. Place
seam side down in the buttered pan. Repeat to form additional rolls until all the

scallop mixture has been used, placing each roll next to the previous one. Brush the tops and ends with melted butter.

Bake at 350° for 40 to 50 minutes, or until the filo is crisp and golden brown. Cut the rolls diagonally before serving. Serve hot with the Wine Sauce.

Wine Sauce

Melt the butter over low heat in a small saucepan. Add the flour and stir until it forms a paste. Stir in the cream, wine, and chicken stock. Stir until the sauce is smooth and slightly thickened. Add salt and pepper to taste.

VEGETABLE BAKE

◆

Serves 6 to 8

1	onion, chopped	½	pound filo leaves, thawed and covered with a damp kitchen towel
2	garlic cloves, minced		
1	bunch broccoli florets		
1	head cauliflower florets	½	cup butter, clarified and melted
4	ounces sliced mushrooms	½	pound cheddar cheese, grated
2	potatoes, peeled and sliced	4	eggs, well beaten
	salt and pepper		

◆

Butter a 7 × 11-inch pan; set aside. Preheat oven to 350°.

Combine the onion, garlic, broccoli, cauliflower, mushrooms, and potatoes in a large bowl. Add salt and pepper to taste and mix thoroughly. Set aside.

Place 1 sheet of filo in the bottom of the buttered pan, folding it to fit. Brush some of the butter on the filo with a pastry brush. Layer a second and a third sheet of filo on top, folding them to fit and brushing each one with butter. Spread the vegetable mixture over the filo. Sprinkle the cheese over the vegetables. Pour the well-beaten eggs over the cheese. Top with 2 or 3 sheets of folded, buttered filo. Before baking, sprinkle a few drops of water over the top and around the edges of the filo to prevent it from curling.

Bake at 350° for 40 to 50 minutes, or until the filo is crisp and golden brown. Serve hot.

PARMESAN-SHRIMP STRUDEL
WITH BECHAMEL SAUCE

Serves 4

Bechamel Sauce
3   tablespoons butter
2   tablespoons flour
1   cup cream (or light cream)
¼   teaspoon nutmeg
    salt and pepper

1   pound shrimp, cooked, peeled,
      and deveined
½   cup onion, chopped
½   cup fresh parsley, chopped

1   cup Parmesan cheese (or
      Romano), grated
    salt and pepper
½   pound filo leaves, thawed and
      covered with a damp
      kitchen towel
½   cup butter, clarified and melted
2   cups bread crumbs, toasted

Butter a 7 × 11-inch pan; set aside. Preheat oven to 350°.

Bechamel Sauce
Melt the butter in a small saucepan over low heat. Stir in the flour and continue stirring until it forms a paste. Stir in the cream and continue stirring until smooth and slightly thickened. Stir in the nutmeg and add salt and pepper to taste. Set aside.

In a medium bowl combine the shrimp, onion, parsley, and cheese. Add salt and pepper to taste and set aside.

Lay 1 sheet of filo on a large plastic cutting board and fold it it half (lengthwise) to form a rectangle. Brush some of the butter on the filo with a pastry brush. Sprinkle ½ cup of bread crumbs on the filo. Center ¾ cup of the shrimp mixture at one end of the filo. Put ¼ cup of sauce on top of it. Roll the mixture jelly roll fashion. Tuck the ends underneath. Place the roll in the buttered dish seam side down. Repeat to form additional rolls until all of the shrimp filling has been used, placing each roll next to the previous one. Brush completely with butter.

Bake at 350° for 40 to 50 minutes, or until the filo is crisp and golden brown. Serve hot with the Bechamel Sauce.

CHICKEN-ARTICHOKE STRUDEL WITH FETA CHEESE SAUCE

◆

Serves 4 to 6

¼ cup margarine	salt and pepper
4 chicken breast halves, skinned, boned and cut into strips	1 pound filo leaves, thawed and covered with a damp kitchen towel
salt and pepper	1 cup butter, clarified and melted
½ onion, chopped	1 cup marinated artichokes, drained
¼ pound mushrooms, sliced	
2 tablespoons butter (or margarine)	¼ pound feta cheese, crumbled
2 tablespoons flour (or cornstarch)	2 ounces Parmesan cheese, grated
¾ cup cream (or light cream)	
¾ cup chicken stock (or bouillon)	

◆

Butter a 7 × 11-inch pan; set aside. Preheat oven to 350°.

Melt the margarine over low heat in a large skillet. Cook the chicken a few minutes until partially done (meat should be slightly pink). Remove from skillet, drain, and set aside. Salt and pepper the chicken to taste. Cook the onion and mushrooms in the drippings a couple of minutes, until partially done (ingredients should be firm). Remove, drain, and set aside.

To make the sauce melt the butter over low heat in a medium, heavy saucepan. Stir in the flour and continue stirring until it forms a paste. Stir in the cream and chicken stock. Stir the mixture until smooth and slightly thickened. Add salt and pepper to taste. Turn off the heat and set aside.

Lay 1 sheet of filo on a large plastic cutting board. Brush some of the butter on the filo with a pastry brush. Center a few chicken strips at one end of the filo. Add ¼ cup of the mushrooms and onion, a few artichoke leaves, 2 tablespoons of feta cheese, and 2 tablespoons Parmesan cheese to the chicken strips. Top with 2 tablespoons of sauce. Fold the sides of the filo over the chicken, sealing in the mixture, and roll up jelly roll fashion. Place the roll seam side down in the buttered dish. Repeat to form additional rolls until all of the chicken has been used, placing each roll next to the previous one. Brush completely with butter.

Bake at 350° for 40 to 50 minutes, or until the filo is crisp and golden brown. Serve hot with the remaining sauce.

THAI SHRIMP BAKE

Serves 5 to 6

¼ cup butter
1 cup green onions, chopped
2 garlic cloves, minced
½ cup green pepper, chopped
1½ pounds shrimp, peeled and
     deveined
½ cup fresh parsley, chopped
1 tablespoon lemon juice
2 teaspoons sugar
1 teaspoon ginger
2 teaspoons chili powder
1 tablespoon curry powder
   salt and pepper
1 tablespoon flour (or cornstarch)

2 cups sour cream
1 cup coconut, grated, divided
1 cup dry-roasted peanuts, divided
½ pound filo leaves, thawed and
     covered with a damp
     kitchen towel
½ cup butter, clarified and melted
2 cups bread crumbs, toasted

Butter a 7 × 11-inch pan; set aside. Preheat oven to 350°.

Melt butter in a medium skillet over low heat. Cook the onion, garlic, green pepper, and shrimp until partially done (ingredients should be firm and meat should be slightly pink). Drain well. Stir in the parsley, lemon juice, sugar, ginger, chili powder, and curry powder and mix thoroughly. Add salt and pepper to taste.

In a small dish, combine the flour and a couple of tablespoons of the sour cream, mixing thoroughly. Add to the onion mixture. Add the rest of the sour cream to the onion mixture, blending thoroughly. Stir in ½ cup coconut and ½ cup peanuts and set aside.

Place 1 sheet of filo in the bottom of the buttered pan, folding it to fit. Brush some of the butter on the filo with a pastry brush. Layer a second and a third sheet of filo on top, folding them to fit and brushing each one with butter. Sprinkle the bread crumbs over the filo. Spread the shrimp mixture over the bread crumbs. Top with 2 or 3 sheets of folded buttered filo. Before baking, sprinkle a few drops of water over the top and around the edges of the filo to prevent it from curling.

Bake at 350° for 40 to 50 minutes, or until the filo is crisp and golden brown. Serve hot with the remaining coconut and peanuts.

❖❖❖

BAYOU SHRIMP CASSEROLE

◆

Serves 4 to 6

½ cup margarine (or 3 tablespoons
      bacon drippings)
1   cup green onions, chopped
1   onion, chopped
2   garlic cloves, minced
1   green pepper, chopped
2   cups okra, chopped
2   bay leaves
½ cup fresh parsley, chopped
2   cups tomatoes, chopped
1   pound shrimp, peeled and
      deveined
     salt and pepper

6   drops Tabasco sauce
2   cups bread crumbs (or
      croutons)*, buttered and
      toasted
½ pound filo leaves, thawed and
      covered with a damp kitchen
      towel
½ cup butter, clarified and melted

◆

Butter a 7 × 11-inch pan; set aside. Preheat oven to 350°.

Melt the margarine (or heat the bacon drippings) in a large skillet. Add the green
onions, onion, garlic, and green pepper. Stir in the okra and bay leaves. Cook about
10 minutes, stirring occasionally. Stir in the parsley, tomatoes, and shrimp and
continue stirring while cooking 2 or 3 more minutes. Remove the bay leaves. Add
salt and pepper to taste. Stir in the Tabasco and mix thoroughly. Set aside.

Place 1 sheet of filo in the bottom of the buttered pan, folding it to fit. Brush some
of the butter on the filo with a pastry brush. Layer a second and a third sheet of filo
on top, folding them to fit and brushing each one with butter. Sprinkle half of the
bread crumbs (or croutons or rice) over the filo. Spread half the shrimp mixture
over the bread crumbs. Top with 2 more sheets of folded, buttered filo. Sprinkle the
remaining bread crumbs (or croutons or rice) on filo and spread the other half of
the shrimp mixture over the bread crumbs. Cover with 2 or 3 folded, buttered
sheets of filo. Before baking, sprinkle a few drops of water over the top and around
the edges of the filo to prevent it from curling.

Bake at 350° for 40 to 50 minutes, or until the filo is crisp and golden brown. Serve
hot.

*2 cups cooked rice may be substituted for the bread crumbs.

❖❖❖

FILO-WRAPPED TURKEY
WITH ORANGE-WALNUT SAUCE

◆

Serves 8 to 10

Orange Sauce

2   cups orange juice
2   tablespoons cornstarch
2   teaspoons sugar
¼   cup fresh parsley, chopped
½   teaspoon orange extract
2   teaspoons orange peel, grated
⅓   cup orange liqueur
    salt and pepper
1   cup walnuts, chopped, divided

2   pounds turkey (or chicken),
    cooked, skinned, boned,
    and sliced
½   pound filo leaves, thawed and
    covered with a damp
    kitchen towel
½   cup butter, clarified and melted

◆

Butter a 9 × 13-inch pan; set aside. Preheat oven to 350°.

Orange Sauce

In a medium saucepan, combine the orange juice and cornstarch. Stir until the cornstarch dissolves. Stir in the sugar, parsley, orange extract, and orange peel. Stir while cooking, over low heat, until sauce is smooth and partially thickened. Stir in the orange liqueur and add salt and pepper to taste. Stir in ¾ cup walnuts. Remove from heat and set aside.

Place 1 sheet of filo in the bottom of the buttered pan, folding it to fit. Brush some of the butter on the filo with a pastry brush. Layer a second and a third sheet of filo on top, folding them to fit and brushing each one with butter. Arrange the sliced turkey over the buttered filo. Cover the turkey with a layer of the orange sauce. Top with 4 or 5 sheets of folded, buttered filo. Sprinkle the rest of the walnuts on top. Before baking, sprinkle a few drops of water over the top and around the edges of the filo to prevent it from curling.

Bake at 350° for 40 to 50 minutes, or until the filo is crisp and golden brown. Serve hot with additional sauce.

CHICKEN, TOMATO, AND FETA-STUFFED FILO

Serves 4 to 5

½　cup flour
4　chicken breast halves, boned, skinned, and cut into strips
¼　cup butter (or margarine)
¼　cup olive oil
1　onion, chopped
2　garlic cloves, minced
15　ounces Italian-style tomato sauce
14　ounces Italian-style stewed tomatoes, drained
½　cup fresh parsley, chopped
¼　cup white wine

½　teaspoon oregano
1　tablespoon sugar
　　salt and pepper
　　cayenne pepper
½　pound feta cheese, crumbled
1　pound filo leaves, thawed and covered with a damp kitchen towel
1　cup butter, clarified and melted

◆

Butter a 7 × 11-inch pan; set aside. Preheat oven to 350°.

Put the flour in a medium bowl and coat the chicken with it. Melt the butter in a large skillet over low heat. Cook the chicken until slightly pink and partially done. Remove the chicken and set aside. Drain the skillet. Heat the olive oil in the skillet over low heat. Cook the onion and garlic for a couple of minutes. Add the tomato sauce, stewed tomatoes, parsley, wine, oregano, and sugar. Add salt, pepper, and cayenne to taste. Simmer a few minutes and reduce. Set aside.

Place 1 sheet of filo in the bottom of the buttered pan, folding it to fit. Brush some of the butter on the filo with a pastry brush. Layer a second and a third sheet of filo on top, folding them to fit and brushing each one with butter. Put the chicken on the filo. Spoon on the tomato mixture and sprinkle the cheese over the tomatoes. Top with 2 or 3 sheets of folded, buttered filo. Before baking, sprinkle a few drops of water over the top and around the edges of the filo to prevent it from curling.

Bake at 350° for 40 to 50 minutes, or until the filo is crisp and golden brown.

CAJUN SHRIMP CASSEROLE

Serves 8 to 10

¼ cup margarine
2 tablespoons olive oil
1 onion, chopped
1 cup green onions, chopped
2 garlic cloves, minced
1 cup green pepper, chopped
½ cup celery, chopped
1 tablespoon chili powder
½ teaspoon oregano
½ teaspoon basil
1 tablespoon sugar
¼ cup burgundy wine
1 tablespoon Worcestershire sauce
15 ounces Cajun-style stewed tomatoes, drained
8 ounces tomato sauce

1 tablespoon cornstarch, dissolved in ¼ cup cold water
½ cup chicken stock (or bouillon)
 salt and pepper
 cayenne pepper
2 pounds shrimp, peeled and deveined
½ pound filo leaves, thawed and covered with a damp kitchen towel
½ cup butter, clarified and melted
2 cups bread crumbs (or cooked rice)

Butter a 9 × 13-inch pan; set aside. Preheat oven to 350°.

Melt the margarine over low heat in a large skillet. Add the olive oil and heat until hot. Add the onion, green onion, garlic, green pepper, and celery and cook, stirring continuously, until tender. Add the chili powder, oregano, basil, sugar, wine, and Worcestershire sauce. Stir in the tomatoes and tomato sauce. Add the cornstarch and chicken stock and simmer over low heat, stirring occasionally, for about 10 minutes until slightly thickened. Add salt, pepper, and cayenne to taste. Stir in the shrimp and continue simmering over low heat, about 5 minutes.

Place 1 sheet of filo in the bottom of the buttered pan, folding it to fit. Brush some of the butter on the filo with a pastry brush. Layer a second and a third sheet of folded, buttered filo on top. Put the bread crumbs (or rice) on the buttered filo. Put the shrimp filling on the bread crumbs, spreading it evenly over the filo. Top with 4 or 5 sheets of folded, buttered filo. Before baking, sprinkle a few drops of water over the top and around the edges of the filo to prevent it from curling.

Bake at 350° for 40 to 50 minutes, or until the filo is crisp and golden brown. Serve hot.

EGGPLANT CASSEROLE

◆

Serves 5 to 7

3 slices bacon	8 ounces tomato paste
1 small eggplant, sliced into ½-inch slices	salt and pepper
½ cup flour	1 pound filo leaves, thawed and covered with a damp kitchen towel
1 onion, chopped	
2 garlic cloves, minced	1 cup butter, clarified and melted
1 green pepper, chopped	2 cups bread crumbs, buttered and toasted
½ cup celery, chopped	
¼ pound mushrooms, sliced	
1 tablespoon sugar	
15 ounces Creole-style stewed tomatoes	

◆

Butter a 7 × 11-inch pan; set aside. Preheat oven to 350°.

Fry the bacon over medium-low heat in a large skillet. While bacon is cooking prepare the eggplant. Put the flour in a medium bowl. Dip and coat the sliced eggplant in the flour. Remove bacon from skillet and drain on paper towels. Cook eggplant in bacon drippings, over medium-low heat, until golden. Remove with a slotted spoon and drain on paper towels.

Cook the onion, garlic, green pepper, celery, and mushrooms, in the drippings, until partially done (ingredients should still be firm); drain well. Stir in the sugar, stewed tomatoes, and tomato paste. Reduce for a few minutes, stirring continuously. Crumble the bacon and stir it into the mixture. Stir in the eggplant. Add salt and pepper to taste.

Place 1 sheet of filo in the bottom of the buttered pan, folding it to fit. Brush some of the butter on the filo with a pastry brush. Layer a second and a third sheet of filo on top folding them to fit and brushing each one with butter. Sprinkle the bread crumbs on the filo. Spread the eggplant mixture over the buttered filo. Top with 2 or 3 sheets of folded, buttered filo. Before baking, sprinkle a few drops of water over the top and around the edges of the filo to prevent it from curling.

Bake at 350° for 40 to 50 minutes, or until the filo is crisp and golden brown. Serve hot.

CHICKEN AND CABBAGE-STUFFED FILO

◆

Serves 4 to 5

2 quarts water	½ cup butter, clarified and melted
1 teaspoon salt	¼ pound Monterey Jack cheese,
6 cabbage leaves	grated
½ cup margarine	
4 chicken breast halves, boned,	***Sauce***
skinned, and cut into two-	2 tablespoons butter
inch strips	1 tablespoon flour (or cornstarch)
½ onion, chopped	1 cup cream (or light cream)
¼ pound mushrooms, sliced	½ cup chicken stock (or bouillon)
salt and pepper	salt and pepper
½ pound filo leaves, thawed and	
covered with a damp	
kitchen towel	

◆

Butter a 7 × 11-inch pan; set aside. Preheat oven to 350°.

Put the water and salt in a large saucepan and bring to a boil. Add the cabbage leaves and simmer over low heat for about 5 minutes to soften. Set aside.

Melt the margarine over low heat in a large skillet. Cook the chicken until partially done (meat should be slightly pink). Remove and set aside. Cook the onions and mushrooms in the drippings for a couple of minutes, until partially done (vegetables should be firm). Remove with a slotted spoon and put on a plate. Season the chicken, onions, and mushrooms to taste with salt and pepper.

Lay 1 sheet of filo on a large plastic cutting board. Fold the filo in half, lengthwise, to form a rectangle. Brush some of the butter on the filo with a pastry brush. Center a cabbage leaf at one end of the filo. Put a few chicken strips and about ½ cup of onion and mushrooms on the filo. Sprinkle a couple of tablespoons of grated cheese on top. Roll up jelly roll fashion. Tuck the ends underneath. Place the roll in the buttered dish seam side down. Repeat to form additional rolls until all the chicken has been used, placing each roll next to the previous one. Brush the roll with butter.

Bake at 350° for 40 to 50 minutes, or until the filo is crisp and golden brown. Serve hot with the sauce.

Sauce

Melt the butter over low heat in a saucepan, add the flour and stir until it forms a paste. Stir in the cream and chicken stock. Stir until the sauce is smooth and slightly thickened. Add salt and pepper to taste.

DILL-RICOTTA PIE

Serves 4 to 5

½ pound feta cheese, crumbled	1 pound filo leaves, thawed and
1 pound ricotta cheese	covered with a damp kitchen
½ pound Monterey Jack cheese,	towel
grated	1 cup butter, clarified and melted
½ cup fresh parsley, chopped	
4 green onions, chopped	
2 teaspoons dill weed (or 2	
tablespoons fresh dill,	
chopped)	
salt and pepper	
3 eggs, well beaten	

◆

Butter an 8 × 8-inch pan; set aside. Preheat oven to 350°.

In a large bowl combine the feta, ricotta, and Monterey Jack.

Stir in the parsley, green onions, and dill weed. Add salt and pepper to taste. Add beaten eggs and mix thoroughly.

Place 1 sheet of filo in the bottom of the buttered pan, folding it to fit. Brush some of the butter on the filo with a pastry brush. Layer a second and a third sheet of filo on top, folding them to fit and brushing each one with butter. Spread the filling on the filo. Top with 2 or 3 sheets of folded, buttered filo. Before baking, sprinkle a few drops of water over the top and around the edges of the filo to prevent it from curling.

Bake at 350° for 40 to 50 minutes, or until the filo is crisp and golden brown. Serve hot.

CHICKEN CORDON BLEU
WITH WINE SAUCE

Serves 8

8	chicken breast halves, skinned and boned	
½	pound filo leaves, thawed and covered with a damp kitchen towel	
½	cup butter, clarified and melted	
½	pound crab meat (fresh or canned), cooked*	
½	pound Swiss cheese, grated	

Wine Sauce

¼	cup butter (or margarine)
½	onion, chopped
½	pound mushrooms, sliced
2	tablespoons butter
1	tablespoon flour (or cornstarch)
½	cup cream (or light cream)
½	cup white wine
1	cup chicken stock (or bouillon)
	salt and pepper

Butter a 9 × 13-inch pan; set aside. Preheat oven to 350°.

Place each chicken breast between 2 pieces of plastic wrap. Pound with a mallet until ¼-inch thick. Set aside.

Lay 1 sheet of filo on a large plastic cutting board. Fold the sheet in half, lengthwise, to form a rectangle. Brush some of the butter on the filo with a pastry brush. Center a chicken breast half at one end of the filo. Put ¼ cup of crab on top of it. Put a couple of tablespoons of cheese on top of the crab. Roll the mixture jelly roll fashion. Tuck the ends underneath. Place the roll in the buttered dish seam side down. Repeat to form additional rolls until all of the chicken has been used, placing each roll next to the previous one. Brush completely with butter.

Bake at 350° for 40 to 50 minutes, or until the filo is crisp and golden brown. Serve hot with the Wine Sauce

Wine Sauce
Melt the butter over low heat in a small skillet. Sautè the onion and mushrooms. Drain well and set aside. Melt the rest of the butter in a saucepan; add the flour and stir until it forms a paste. Stir in the cream, wine, and chicken stock. Stir until smooth and partially thickened. Add the sautèed mushrooms and onion. Add salt and pepper to taste.

*Substitute 2 ounces of thinly sliced ham for the crab, if desired.

TROPICAL CHICKEN STRUDEL

◆

Serves 4

½ cup margarine	¼ cup soy sauce
4 chicken breast halves, boned and skinned	1 teaspoon ginger
	1 cup coconut, grated
½ cup green onion, chopped	1 cup almonds, toasted and slivered
½ cup green pepper, sliced	½ pound filo leaves, thawed and
½ pound mushrooms, sliced	covered with a damp
salt and pepper	kitchen towel
1 tablespoon cornstarch (or flour)	½ cup butter, clarified and melted
½ cup cream of coconut*	
½ cup chicken stock or bouillon	

◆

Butter a 7 × 11-inch pan; set aside. Preheat oven to 350°.

Melt the margarine in a large skillet over low heat. Cook the chicken, onions, pepper, and mushrooms until partially done (ingredients should still be firm and meat should be slightly pink). Remove the cooked ingredients with a slotted spoon and place on a plate. Add salt and pepper to taste.

Stir the cornstarch into the drippings in the skillet, creating a thick paste. Stir in the cream of coconut, chicken stock, soy sauce, and ginger. Continue stirring while cooking over low heat until sauce is smooth and slightly thickened. Stir in the coconut and almonds and add salt and pepper to taste. Remove from heat and set aside.

Lay 2 sheets of filo on a large plastic cutting board. Fold in half, lengthwise, to form a rectangle. Brush some of the butter on the filo with a pastry brush. Center a chicken breast half, topped with some of the mushrooms, onions, and peppers at one end of the filo. Put about 2 tablespoons of sauce on the chicken. Roll the filo sheets in a jelly roll fashion. Tuck the ends underneath. Place the roll in the buttered pan seam side down. Repeat to form 4 more rolls, placing the roll next to the previous one. Brush completely with butter.

Bake at 350° for 40 to 50 minutes, or until the filo is crisp and golden brown. Serve hot with remaining sauce at the table.

*Cream of coconut is found in the beverage section of your supermarket.

❖❖❖

FILO-WRAPPED PASTA CARBONA

◆

Serves 4 to 6

3 ounces spaghetti, broken into
    1-inch pieces
2 quarts boiling, salted water
½ pound bacon, preferably Italian,
    cut into 2-inch strips
1 onion, chopped
2 garlic cloves, minced
¼ cup white wine
4 ounces Parmesan cheese, freshly
    grated

½ cup fresh parsley, chopped
    salt and pepper
3 eggs, well beaten
2 cups bread crumbs, buttered and
    toasted
½ pound filo leaves, thawed and
    covered with a damp
    kitchen towel
½ cup butter, clarified and melted

◆

Butter a 7 × 11-inch pan; set aside. Preheat oven to 350°.

Cook the spaghetti in the boiling, salted water for 10 to 12 minutes, until tender but still firm, drain and set aside.

In a medium skillet cook the bacon over low heat until done but not crisp. Remove with a slotted spoon to a plate. Sautè the onion and garlic in the drippings for a couple of minutes. Drain well. Add the wine and simmer for a couple of minutes. Stir in the Parmesan cheese and parsley. Add salt and pepper to taste. Stir in the bacon and eggs, mixing thoroughly. Stir in the spaghetti. Set aside.

Place 1 sheet of filo in the bottom of the buttered pan, folding it to fit. Brush some of the butter on the filo with a pastry brush. Layer a second and a third sheet of filo on top, folding them to fit and brushing each one with butter. Sprinkle the bread crumbs over the filo. Spoon on the spaghetti mixture. Top with 2 or 3 sheets of folded, buttered filo. Before baking, sprinkle a few drops of water over the top and around the edges of the filo to prevent it from curling.

Bake at 350° for 40 to 50 minutes, or until the filo is crisp and golden brown. Serve hot.

DAZZLING
DESSERTS

CHERRY-ALMOND STRUDEL

♦

Makes 16 to 18 2-inch servings

2 pounds dark sweet cherries, pitted	1½ cups bread cubes, buttered and toasted, divided
1 cup almonds, toasted and coarsely ground	1 pound filo leaves, thawed and covered with a damp kitchen towel
1 cup cherry preserves	1 cup butter, clarified and melted
1 tablespoon cornstarch	powdered sugar for dusting
1 teaspoon lemon zest, grated	
2 teaspoons almond extract	

♦

Butter a 9 × 13-inch pan; set aside. Preheat oven to 350°.

In a large bowl combine the cherries and almonds. Put the preserves in a small bowl and stir in the cornstarch, lemon zest, and almond extract. Add the preserve mixture to the cherries and almonds, stirring well. Set aside.

Lay 1 sheet of filo on a large plastic cutting board. Brush some of the butter on the filo with a pastry brush. Layer a second and a third sheet of filo on top, brushing each one with butter. Sprinkle ½ cup of the bread cubes over the buttered filo. Put 1 cup of the cherry-almond mixture in a long, narrow row at short end of the filo. Roll up jelly roll fashion. Tuck the ends underneath. Place the roll seam side down in the buttered pan. Repeat to form additional rolls until all the filling is used, placing each roll next to the previous one. Brush the tops and ends with the remaining melted butter.

Bake at 350° for 40 to 50 minutes, or until the filo is crisp and golden brown. Cool on wire rack. Dust with powdered sugar. Cut the rolls diagonally and serve warm or cold. Serve with whipped cream or ice cream, if desired.

STRAWBERRY AND BLUEBERRY TART

Makes 8 2-inch servings

½ cup butter, melted
1¼ cups sugar
6 eggs
2 teaspoons vanilla extract
1 teaspoon lemon extract
2 tablespoons white vinegar
½ pound filo leaves, thawed and
    covered with a damp
    kitchen towel
½ cup butter, clarified and melted
1 cup fresh strawberries, washed,
    hulled, and sliced
1 cup blueberries (fresh or canned)

Glaze

1 tablespoon cornstarch
½ cup water
½ cup sugar
1 tablespoon butter
1 pint fresh strawberries, washed,
    hulled, and sliced, divided
1 teaspoon almond extract
½ cup blueberries (fresh or canned)

Butter a 7 × 11-inch pan; set aside. Preheat oven to 325°.

To make the custard, combine the melted butter, sugar, and eggs in a large mixing bowl, beating with a mixer. Stir in the vanilla extract, lemon extract, and vinegar. Set aside.

Place 1 sheet of filo in the bottom of the buttered pan, folding it to fit. Brush some of the butter on the filo with a pastry brush. Layer a second and a third sheet of filo on top, folding them to fit and brushing each one with butter. Layer the strawberries and blueberries on the filo. Pour the custard mixture over the fruit, spreading it out evenly. Top with 2 or 3 folded, buttered sheets of filo. Before baking, sprinkle a few drops of water over the top and around the edges of the filo to prevent it from curling.

Bake at 325° for 50 to 60 minutes, or until the custard is set, and the filo is golden brown and crisp. Place on a wire rack while making the glaze.

Glaze

In a saucepan dissolve the cornstarch in the water. Stir in the sugar, butter, and a little more than half of the strawberries. Continue stirring over low heat until the mixture thickens. Remove the cooked berries with a slotted spoon. Stir in the almond extract. After the tart has cooled put the rest of the sliced strawberries and the blueberries on the top. Pour the glaze over the berries. Serve warm or cold.

MANGO-PAPAYA PUFFS

◆

Makes 8 3-inch servings

2	cups cream (or light cream)	½	cup coconut, grated
¼	cup cornstarch	½	pound filo leaves, thawed and
⅛	teaspoon salt		covered with a damp
¼	cup butter		kitchen towel
¾	cup sugar	½	cup butter, clarified and melted
6	egg yolks		
2	teaspoons vanilla extract		*Glaze*
2	teaspoons orange extract	1	tablespoon butter
2	tablespoons orange liqueur	¼	cup orange marmalade
1	mango, peeled and sliced	½	cup powdered sugar
1	papaya, peeled and sliced	¼	cup coconut, grated
1	banana, peeled and sliced		
½	cup crushed pineapple		

◆

Butter a 7 × 11-inch pan; set aside. Preheat oven to 350°.

In a double boiler, combine the cream, cornstarch, and salt. Stir until the cornstarch dissolves. Stir in the butter and sugar. Cook over—not immersed in—boiling water. Continue stirring until the butter melts. In a small mixing bowl, beat egg yolks well; stir in 2 tablespoons of the hot mixture and mix thoroughly. Stir the yolk mixture into the heated custard. Continue stirring until smooth and partially thickened. Stir in the vanilla extract, orange extract, and liqueur. Remove from heat and set aside.

Place 1 sheet of filo in the bottom of the buttered pan, folding it to fit. Brush some of the butter on the filo with a pastry brush. Layer a second and a third sheet of filo on top, folding them to fit the pan and brushing each one with butter. Layer the fruit over the filo. Pour the custard over the fruit. Top with 2 or 3 folded, buttered sheets of filo. Before baking, sprinkle a few drops of water over the top and around the edges of the filo to prevent it from curling.

Bake at 350° for 40 to 50 minutes, or until the custard is set and the filo is golden brown and crisp. Cool on a wire rack while making the glaze.

Glaze
Melt the butter over low heat in a small saucepan. Stir in the marmalade and powdered sugar. Continue stirring until smooth, hot, and bubbly. Stir in the coconut. Spread the glaze over the filo. Serve warm or cold.

BASIC BAKLAVA

Makes 48 to 50 2-inch servings

Syrup

3 cups sugar
1½ cups water
2 tablespoons lemon juice
2 tablespoons rose water*
½ cup honey

Filling

2 cups walnuts, ground
2 cups almonds, ground
2 cups coconut, grated

3 tablespoons sugar
2 teaspoons cinnamon
3 tablespoons rose water*

1 pound filo leaves, thawed and covered with a damp kitchen towel
1½ cups butter, clarified and melted

Butter an 11 × 13-inch jelly roll pan; set aside. Preheat oven to 350°.

Syrup

In a large, heavy saucepan combine the sugar, water, lemon juice, and rose water. Stir over low heat until the sugar dissolves. Bring the syrup to a boil, then turn the heat down and simmer for 20 to 25 minutes. Stir in the honey. Let the syrup cool while making the filling.

Filling

In a large bowl combine the walnuts, almonds, and coconut. In a cup mix the sugar, cinnamon, and rose water; pour over the nut mixture and mix thoroughly.

Place 1 sheet of filo in the bottom of the buttered pan. Brush some of the butter on the filo with a pastry brush. Layer 7 more sheets of buttered filo in the pan. Put about ⅓ of the nut mixture on the buttered filo, spreading it evenly. Cover the nut layer with 3 more sheets of buttered filo. Put half of the remaining filling on the filo, also spreading it evenly. Top with 3 more sheets of buttered filo. Spread the rest of the nut mixture on top. Top with 6 or 7 sheets of filo, buttering each sheet. Cut the top layers of the filo diagonally before baking. Before baking, sprinkle a few drops of water over the top and around the edges of the filo, to prevent it from curling.

Bake at 350° for 40 to 50 minutes, or until the filo is crisp and golden brown. Pour the cool syrup over the hot baklava. When cool, cut through the bottom layers

*Rose water is found in Middle Eastern or specialty food stores.

of the previously cut filo. Rotate the pan one-quarter of a turn and cut the filo in straight rows to make diamond-shaped servings. Cool thoroughly, then cover before storing.

NOTE: Baklava freezes well and is better if made a day ahead.

WHITE CHOCOLATE WONDER

◆

Makes 15 2-inch servings

10 ounces white chocolate	½ pound filo leaves, thawed and covered with a damp kitchen towel
24 ounces cream cheese, at room temperature	
½ cup sour cream	½ cup butter, clarified and melted
¾ cup sugar	
1 tablespoon vanilla extract	***Topping***
3 egg yolks	2 tablespoons sour cream
2 ounces white chocolate liqueur	2 ounces white chocolate

◆

Butter a 7 × 11-inch pan; set aside. Preheat oven to 350°.

Break the white chocolate into small pieces and melt in a double boiler over low heat, stirring until smooth. In a large bowl combine the cream cheese, sour cream, sugar, vanilla extract, and egg yolks. Beat with an electric mixer until creamy. Stir in the melted chocolate and liqueur and blend well. Set aside.

Place 1 sheet of filo in the bottom of the buttered pan, folding it to fit. Brush some of the butter on the filo with a pastry brush. Layer a second and a third sheet of filo on top, folding them to fit and brushing each one with butter. Spoon the mixture onto the filo, spreading it evenly. Top with 2 or 3 sheets of folded, buttered filo. Brush the top with the remaining melted butter. Before baking, sprinkle a few drops of water over the top and around the edges of the filo to prevent it from curling.

Bake at 350° for 40 to 50 minutes, or until the filo is crisp and golden brown. Cool thoroughly on a wire rack while making the topping.

Topping
Melt the white chocolate in a double boiler over low heat, stirring until smooth. Stir the sour cream into the melted chocolate. Drizzle the chocolate mixture over the filo, creating a design. Chill. Serve cold.

ORANGE-CHOCOLATE TREAT

◆

Makes 12 2-inch servings

24 ounces cream cheese, at room
　　temperature, divided
¾ cup sugar, divided
1 teaspoon vanilla extract
2 egg yolks, divided
1 cup semisweet chocolate chips
¼ cup sour cream
¼ cup orange liqueur
2 teaspoons orange extract
1 tablespoon cornstarch
2 tablespoons orange juice
　　concentrate, thawed
1 drop orange food coloring

1 pound filo leaves, thawed and
　　covered with a damp
　　kitchen towel
1 cup butter, clarified and melted

Glaze

½ cup powdered sugar
2 tablespoons orange juice
　　concentrate, thawed

Additional Toppings

⅓ cup semisweet chocolate chips
1 tablespoon sour cream
1 tablespoon powdered sugar

◆

Butter a 7 × 11-inch pan; set aside. Preheat oven to 350°.

In a medium bowl combine 12 ounces of the cream cheese, ½ cup of the sugar, the vanilla extract, and 1 egg yolk. Beat with an electric mixer until thoroughly blended. Melt the chocolate in a double boiler over low heat, stirring until smooth. Add the sour cream and melted chocolate chips to the cream cheese mixture, and beat with the mixer until thoroughly blended. Set aside.

In another medium bowl, combine the remaining cream cheese, sugar, and egg yolk. Add the orange liqueur, orange extract, cornstarch, orange juice, and food coloring. Mix thoroughly with a mixer and set aside.

Place 1 sheet of filo in the bottom of the buttered pan, folding it to fit. Brush some of the butter on the filo with a pastry brush. Layer a second and a third sheet of filo on top, folding them to fit and brushing each one with butter. Spread the chocolate mixture evenly on the filo. Layer two folded, buttered sheets of filo over the chocolate. Put the orange mixture on, spreading it evenly. Top with 2 or 3 sheets of folded, buttered filo. Before baking, sprinkle a few drops of water over the top and around the edges of the filo to prevent it from curling.

Bake at 350° for 40 to 50 minutes, or until the filo is crisp and golden brown. Cool thoroughly on a wire rack while making the glaze. Serve cold with Glaze.

Glaze
Combine the powdered sugar and orange juice in a small saucepan. Stir over low heat until smooth, hot and bubbly. Drizzle the glaze over the cooled filo.

Additional Toppings

Melt the chocolate in a double boiler over low heat, stirring until smooth. Stir the sour cream into the melted chocolate. Stir in the powdered sugar and mix thoroughly. Drizzle the melted chocolate over the filo creating a design.

PLUM DELICIOUS SQUARES

◆

Makes 10 3-inch servings

2 cups plums, about 10 to 12, peeled and sliced	½ pound filo leaves, thawed and covered with a damp kitchen towel
¾ cup sugar	
½ cup raisins	½ cup butter, clarified and melted
¼ cup peach schnapps	
2 tablespoons cornstarch	*Glaze*
½ teaspoon cinnamon	1 tablespoon butter
⅛ teaspoon nutmeg	¼ cup peach preserves
1 teaspoon lemon extract	½ cup powdered sugar
½ cup walnuts, chopped	¼ cup walnuts, chopped
2 cups bread crumbs	

◆

Butter a 7 × 11-inch pan; set aside. Preheat oven to 350°.

In a large bowl combine the plums, sugar, raisins, schnapps, cornstarch, cinnamon, nutmeg, and lemon extract. Stir in the walnuts and bread crumbs. Stir until thoroughly mixed. Set aside.

Place 1 sheet of filo in the bottom of the buttered pan, folding it to fit. Brush some of the butter on the filo with a pastry brush. Layer a second and a third sheet of filo on top, folding them to fit and brushing each one with butter. Spread the plum mixture evenly on the buttered filo. Top with 2 or 3 sheets of folded, buttered filo. Before baking, sprinkle a few drops of water over the top and around the edges of the filo to prevent it from curling.

Bake at 350° for 40 to 50 minutes, or until the filo is crisp and golden brown. Cool on a wire rack while making the glaze. Serve warm, with whipped cream or ice cream, if desired.

Glaze

Melt the butter over low heat in a small saucepan. Stir in the peach preserves and powdered sugar. Continue stirring until hot and bubbly. Sprinkle the walnuts over the filo. Pour the glaze over the filo.

GOOSEBERRY-RAISIN ROLLS

Makes 6 2-inch servings

2 cups gooseberries (fresh or canned) well drained
1 cup raisins
½ cup pecans, chopped
¾ cup sugar
2 tablespoons cornstarch
2 teaspoons vanilla extract
2 teaspoons orange extract
2 tablespoons orange liqueur
½ pound filo leaves, thawed and covered with a damp kitchen towel

½ cup butter, clarified and melted
2 cups bread crumbs, toasted
powdered sugar (optional)

Glaze

¼ cup orange marmalade
½ cup powdered sugar
2 tablespoons pecans, chopped

Butter a 6 × 10-inch pan; set aside. Preheat oven to 350°.

In a medium bowl combine the gooseberries, raisins, pecans, sugar, and cornstarch. Mix thoroughly, but do not over beat. Stir in the vanilla extract, orange extract, and orange liqueur. Stir in the bread crumbs, do not over beat.

Lay 1 sheet of filo on a large plastic cutting board. Brush some of the butter on the filo with a pastry brush. Layer a second and a third sheet of filo on top, brushing each with butter. Put 1 cup of gooseberry mixture in a long, narrow row across the short end of the filo. Roll up jelly roll fashion. Tuck the ends underneath. Place the roll seam side down in the buttered pan. Repeat to form additional rolls until all the filling is used, placing each roll next to the previous one. Brush the tops and ends with the remaining melted butter.

Bake at 350° for 40 to 50 minutes, or until the filo is crisp and golden brown. Cool on wire rack. Dust with powdered sugar, if desired, or top with the glaze.

Glaze
Combine the orange marmalade and powdered sugar in a small saucepan. Stir over low heat until hot and bubbly. Spread the warm glaze on the warm filo. Sprinkle the pecans over the top. Cut the rolls diagonally before serving. Serve warm or cold. Served with whipped cream or ice cream, if desired.

PEAR-APPLE STRUDEL

◆

Makes 8 to 10 2-inch servings

2	cups pears, peeled and sliced	½	cup butter, clarified and melted
2	cups apples, peeled and sliced		powdered sugar (optional)
½	cup raisins		
½	cup walnuts, chopped		***Orange Glaze***
¾	cup sugar	1	tablespoon butter
2	cups bread crumbs	¼	cup orange marmalade
¼	cup orange liqueur	½	cup powdered sugar
2	teaspoons vanilla extract	2	tablespoons walnuts, chopped
2	teaspoons orange extract		
½	pound filo leaves, thawed and covered with a damp kitchen towel		

◆

Butter a 7 × 11-inch pan; set aside. Preheat oven to 350°.

In a large bowl combine the pears, apples, raisins, walnuts and sugar. Stir in the bread crumbs and mix thoroughly. In a little dish mix the orange liqueur, vanilla extract, and orange extract. Stir this into the fruit mixture.

Lay 1 sheet of filo on a large plastic cutting board. Brush some of the butter on the filo with a pastry brush. Layer a second and a third sheet of filo on top, brushing each one with butter. Put 1 cup of the mixture in a long, narrow row at the short end of the filo. Roll up jelly roll fashion. Tuck the ends underneath. Place the roll seam side down in the buttered pan. Repeat to form additional rolls until all the filling is used, placing each roll next to the previous one. Brush the tops and ends with the remaining melted butter.

Bake at 350° for 40 to 50 minutes, or until the filo is crisp and golden brown. Cool on a wire rack. Dust with powdered sugar, if desired, or top with the glaze.

Orange Glaze

Melt the butter over low heat in a small saucepan. Stir in the orange marmalade and powdered sugar. Continue stirring until hot and bubbly. Spread the hot glaze on the warm filo. Sprinkle the walnuts on the top. Cut the rolls diagonally before serving. Serve warm or cold. Serve with whipped cream or ice cream, if desired.

APPLE-NUT BAKLAVA

Makes 20 to 25 2-inch servings

Syrup
1½ cups sugar
1 cup water
2 tablespoons lemon juice
2 tablespoons rose water*
1 cup honey

Filling
2 cups apples, peeled and grated
1 cup walnuts, ground
1 cup almonds, ground
1 cup coconut, grated

½ cup raisins
½ cup sugar
2 teaspoons cinnamon
½ teaspoon nutmeg
¼ teaspoon cloves
2 teaspoons lemon peel, grated
3 tablespoons rose water*
1 pound filo leaves, thawed and covered with a damp kitchen towel
1 cup butter, clarified and melted

Butter a 7 × 11-inch pan; set aside. Preheat oven to 350°.

Syrup
In a large, heavy saucepan combine the sugar, water, lemon juice, and rose water. Stir over low heat until the sugar dissolves. Bring the syrup to a boil, then turn the heat down and simmer for 20 to 25 minutes. Stir in the honey. Let cool while making the filling.

Filling
In a large bowl combine the apples, walnuts, almonds, coconut, and raisins. In a small bowl combine the sugar, cinnamon, nutmeg, cloves, lemon peel, and rose water; pour over the apple nut mixture and mix thoroughly.

Place 1 sheet of filo in the bottom of the buttered pan, folding it to fit. Brush some of the butter on the filo with a pastry brush. Layer 2 or 3 more sheets of folded, buttered filo in the pan. Put about one-third of the mixture on the buttered filo, spreading it evenly. Put 3 more sheets of folded, buttered, filo over the apple nut mixture. Put half of the remaining filling on the filo, also spreading it evenly. Top with 3 more sheets of folded, buttered filo. Spread on the rest of the apple-nut mixture. Cover with 3 or 4 sheets of folded, buttered filo. Cut the top layers of the filo diagonally before baking. Before baking, sprinkle a few drops of water over the top and around the edges of the filo to prevent it from curling.

Bake at 350° for 40 to 50 minutes, or until the filo is crisp and golden brown. Pour the cool syrup over the hot apple baklava. When cool, complete the previously

*Rose water is found in Middle Eastern and specialty food stores.

begun diagonal cuts by cutting through the bottom layers of the baklava. Rotate the pan one-quarter of a turn and cut the filo in straight rows to make diamond-shaped servings. Cover before storing.

Note: This dessert is better if made a day ahead.

MINI BLUEBERRY-CHEESE ROLLS

◆

Makes 10 to 12 2-inch servings

8 ounces cream cheese, at room temperature	½ pound filo leaves, thawed and covered with a damp kitchen towel
¼ cup sugar	½ cup butter, clarified and melted
2 teaspoons cornstarch	
3 tablespoons heavy cream	***Glaze***
2 egg yolks	1 tablespoon butter
1 teaspoon lemon extract	½ cup blueberry preserves
1 teaspoon vanilla extract	¼ cup powdered sugar
¼ cup blueberries (fresh, frozen, or canned), well drained	⅓ cup blueberries, (fresh, frozen, or canned), well drained

◆

Butter a 6 × 10-inch pan; set aside. Preheat oven to 350°.

In a medium bowl beat the cream cheese, sugar, cornstarch, cream, egg yolks, lemon extract, and vanilla extract, with an electric mixer until creamy. Stir in the blueberries. Set aside.

Lay 1 sheet of filo on a large plastic cutting board. Fold the sheet of filo in half, lengthwise, to form a rectangle. Brush some of the butter on the filo with a pastry brush. Put about ¾ cup of the filling in a long, narrow row down the long end of the filo. Roll up jelly roll fashion. Tuck the ends underneath. Place the roll seam side down in the buttered pan. Repeat to form additional rolls until all the filling is used, placing each roll next to the previous one. Brush tops and ends with the remaining melted butter.

Bake at 350° for 40 to 50 minutes, or until the filo is crisp and golden brown. Place on a wire rack while making the glaze.

Glaze
In a small saucepan melt the butter over low heat. Stir in the preserves and powdered sugar and mix thoroughly. Add the blueberries and continue stirring until hot and bubbly. Spread the glaze over the warm filo. Serve warm or cold. Cut diagonally before serving.

❖❖❖

CHOCOLATE, HONEY, AND FIG FILO

◆

Makes 20 to 25 2-inch servings

Syrup

1½	cups sugar
¾	cup water
2	tablespoons lemon juice
2	teaspoons orange extract
2	tablespoons cocoa
¾	cup honey

Filling

12	ounces figs, finely chopped
1	cup walnuts, ground
1	cup almonds, ground

½	cup sugar
1	teaspoon cinnamon
8	ounces chocolate chips
1	pound filo leaves, thawed and covered with a damp kitchen towel
1	cup butter, clarified and melted

Topping

2	ounces chocolate chips
2	tablespoons sour cream

◆

Butter a 7 × 11-inch pan; set aside. Preheat oven to 350°.

Syrup

In a large heavy saucepan combine the sugar, water, lemon juice, orange extract, and cocoa. Stir over low heat, until the sugar dissolves. Bring the syrup to a boil, then turn the heat down, and simmer for 20 to 25 minutes. Stir in the honey. Let cool while making the filling.

Filling

In a large bowl combine the figs, walnuts, and almonds. Mix the sugar and cinnamon in a cup and pour over the fruit and nut mixture; mix thoroughly. Melt the chocolate chips in a double boiler over low heat, stirring continuously until smooth. Add the melted chocolate to the fruit and nut mixture, stirring until completely blended. Set aside.

Lay 1 sheet of filo on a large plastic cutting board. Brush some of the butter on the filo with a pastry brush. Layer a second and a third sheet of folded, buttered filo on top of the first sheet. Put 1 cup of the filling in a long, narrow row at the short end of filo. Roll up jelly roll fashion. Place seam side down in the buttered pan. Repeat to form additional rolls until all the filling is used, placing each roll next to the previous one. Butter the tops and sides of the rolls with the remaining butter. Cut the top layers of filo diagonally before baking.

Bake at 350° for 40 to 50 minutes, or until the filo is crisp and golden brown. Pour the cool syrup over the hot filo. Cool on a wire rack while making the topping.

Topping

Melt the chocolate in a double boiler over low heat, stirring until smooth. Stir the sour cream into the melted chocolate. Drizzle the chocolate over the rolls. Cover before storing.

NOTE: This dessert is better if made a day ahead.

RASPBERRY-ALMOND STRUDEL

◆

Makes 8 3-inch servings

1 pint raspberries (well drained if frozen)	½ pound filo leaves, thawed and covered with a damp kitchen towel
2 tablespoons amaretto	
½ cup almonds, toasted and chopped or slivered	½ cup butter, clarified and melted
¾ cup sugar	***Glaze***
2 teaspoons almond extract	2 teaspoons cornstarch
1 teaspoon vanilla extract	4 ounces raspberry jam
1 teaspoon lemon extract	2 tablespoons amaretto
2 cups bread crumbs	¼ cup almonds, toasted and chopped or slivered

◆

Butter a 7 × 11-inch pan; set aside. Preheat oven to 350°.

In a medium bowl combine the raspberries, amaretto, almonds, and sugar. Stir in the almond, vanilla and lemon extracts. Set aside.

Place 1 sheet of filo in the bottom of the buttered pan, folding it to fit. Brush some of the butter on the filo with a pastry brush. Layer a second and a third sheet of filo on top, folding them to fit and brushing each one with butter. Sprinkle the bread crumbs over the filo. Spread the raspberry mixture over the bread crumbs. Top with 2 or 3 sheets of folded, buttered filo. Before baking, sprinkle a few drops of water over the top and around the edges of the filo to prevent it from curling.

Bake at 350° for 40 to 50 minutes, or until the filo is crisp and golden brown. Cool on a wire rack while making the glaze.

Glaze

In a small saucepan mix the cornstarch and raspberry jam thoroughly. Stir in the amaretto. Continue stirring over low heat until thickened. Sprinkle the almonds over the filo. Spread the glaze over the filo. Serve warm or cold.

HONEY-NUT KATAIFE

Makes 10 to 12 2-inch servings

Syrup
1½ cups sugar
¾ cup water
2 tablespoons lemon juice
¾ cup honey

Filling
1 cup walnuts, ground
1 cup almonds, ground
1 cup pecans, ground

¼ cup sugar
2 teaspoons cinnamon

½ pound filo leaves, thawed and covered with a damp kitchen towel
1 cup butter, clarified and melted
½ pound kataife, thawed, divided and covered with a damp kitchen towel*

Butter a 7 × 11-inch pan; set aside. Preheat oven to 350°.

Syrup
In a large, heavy saucepan combine the sugar, water, and lemon juice. Stir over low heat until the sugar dissolves. Bring the syrup to a boil, then turn the heat down and simmer for 20 minutes. Stir in the honey. Let cool while making the filling.

Filling
In a medium bowl combine the walnuts, almonds, and pecans. Mix the sugar and cinnamon in a cup; stir into the nuts and mix thoroughly. Set aside.

Place 1 sheet of filo in the bottom of the buttered pan, folding it to fit. Brush some of the butter on the filo with a pastry brush. Layer 2 or 3 more sheets of folded, buttered filo in the pan. Layer ½ of the kataife over the filo in the bottom of the pan. Brush some of the butter on the kataife with a pastry brush. Carefully spread the filling over the kataife. Cover the filling with the remaining kataife. Butter the top of the kataife. Top with 2 or 3 sheets of folded, buttered filo. Cut the top layers of the filo diagonally before baking. Sprinkle a few drops of water over the top and around the edges of the filo to prevent it from curling while baking.

Bake at 350° for 40 to 50 minutes, or until the filo is crisp and golden brown. Pour the cool syrup over the hot filo. When cool, complete the previously begun diagonal cuts, by cutting through the bottom layers of the filo. Rotate the pan one-quarter of a turn and cut the filo in straight rows to form diamond-shaped servings. Cover before storing.

Note: This dessert is better if made a day ahead.

*Kataife is shredded filo dough and is found in Middle Eastern and specialty food stores.

MOCHA EXTRAORDINAIRE

◆

Makes 8 2-inch servings

16 ounces cream cheese, at room
    temperature
⅔ cup sugar
2 egg yolks
1 teaspoon instant coffee, dissolved
    in 1 teaspoon hot water
2 tablespoons coffee-flavored
    liqueur
½ cup semisweet chocolate
    chips
2 tablespoons sour cream

½ pound filo leaves, thawed and
    covered with a damp
    kitchen towel
½ cup butter, clarified and melted

Glaze
1 tablespoon butter
1 tablespoon hot water
1 tablespoon coffee-flavored liqueur
1 teaspoon cocoa powder
½ cup powdered sugar

◆

Butter an 8 × 8-inch pan; set aside. Preheat oven to 350°.

In a large bowl beat the cream cheese, sugar, and egg yolks with an electric mixer.
Put half of this mixture in a smaller bowl.

Stir the dissolved coffee into the coffee liqueur. Add the coffee mixture to the
ingredients in the smaller bowl, stirring well, and set aside.

Melt chocolate chips in a double boiler set over low heat, stirring until smooth. Stir
the sour cream into the melted chocolate. Combine the chocolate and cream
cheese mixtures in the large bowl and mix thoroughly; set aside.

Place 1 sheet of filo in the bottom of the buttered pan, folding it to fit. Brush some
of the butter on the filo with a pastry brush. Layer a second and a third sheet of
filo on top, folding them to fit and brushing each one with butter. Spread the
chocolate mixture on the filo. Layer 2 sheets of folded, buttered filo over the
chocolate mixture. Spread the coffee mixture on top. Cover with 2 or 3 sheets of
folded, buttered filo. Before baking, sprinkle a few drops of water over the top
and around the edges of the filo to prevent it from curling.

Bake at 350° for 40 to 50 minutes, or until the custard is set and the filo is crisp and
golden brown. Cool on a wire rack while making the glaze.

Glaze
Melt the butter over low heat in a small saucepan. Stir in the water, liqueur, cocoa,
and powdered sugar, mixing thoroughly. Continue stirring until hot and bubbly.
Drizzle the glaze on the filo creating a design. Serve cold.

APRICOT CUSTARD SQUARES

Makes 6 3-inch servings

2 cups dried apricots, finely chopped	2 teaspoons orange extract
¼ cup apricot liqueur (or other fruit liqueur)	½ cup apricot preserves
2 cups cream (or light cream)	½ pound filo leaves, thawed and covered with a damp kitchen towel
¼ cup cornstarch	½ cup butter, clarified and melted
⅛ teaspoon salt	
¼ cup butter	***Glaze***
⅓ cup sugar	2 tablespoons butter
6 egg yolks	¾ cup apricot preserves
2 teaspoons vanilla extract	¼ cup almonds, slivered
1 teaspoon lemon extract	

Butter a 7 × 11-inch pan; set aside. Preheat oven to 350°.

Put the chopped apricots in a small bowl and pour the liqueur over them. Let apricots soak while making the custard. In a double boiler, combine the cream, cornstarch, and salt. Stir until the cornstarch dissolves. Stir in the butter and sugar. Cook over—not immersed in—boiling water. Continue stirring until the butter melts. In a small mixing bowl, beat egg yolks well; stir in 2 tablespoons of the hot mixture and mix thoroughly. Stir the yolk mixture into the heated custard. Continue stirring until smooth and partially thickened. Stir in the vanilla, lemon and orange extracts, preserves, and the apricot-liqueur mixture. Mix thoroughly, remove from heat, and set aside.

Place 1 sheet of filo in the bottom of the buttered pan, folding it to fit. Brush some of the butter on the filo with a pastry brush. Layer 3 or 4 more sheets of folded, buttered filo on top. Spread the custard over the filo. Top with 3 or 4 folded, buttered sheets of filo. Before baking, sprinkle a few drops of water over the top and around the edges of the filo to prevent it from curling.

Bake at 350° for 40 to 50 minutes, or until the custard is set and the filo is golden brown and crisp. Cool on a wire rack while making the glaze.

Glaze
Melt the butter in a small saucepan over low heat. Stir in the preserves and continue stirring until hot and bubbly. Sprinkle the almonds over the filo then drizzle the glaze over them. Serve warm or cold.

GRASSHOPPER FILO PIE

◆

Makes 8 2-inch servings

16 ounces cream cheese, at room temperature	½ pound filo leaves, thawed and covered with a damp kitchen towel
½ cup sugar	½ cup butter, clarified and melted
2 egg yolks	
¼ cup crème de menthe (green)	***Glaze***
¼ cup crème de cacao	1 tablespoon butter
½ cup semisweet chocolate chips	1 teaspoon cocoa powder
2 tablespoons sour cream	½ cup powdered sugar

◆

Butter a 7 × 11-inch pan; set aside. Preheat oven to 350°.

In a large bowl put the cream cheese, sugar, and egg yolks. Beat with an electric mixer until creamy. Put half of the cream cheese mixture in a smaller bowl.

Add the crème de menthe to the cream cheese mixture in the smaller bowl and mix thoroughly. Set aside.

Stir the crème de cacao into the cream cheese mixture in the larger bowl and mix thoroughly. Melt the chocolate chips in a double boiler over low heat, stirring until smooth. Stir the sour cream into the melted chocolate chips. Stir the chocolate chip mixture into the crème de cacao mixture and mix thoroughly. Set aside.

Place 1 sheet of filo in the bottom of the buttered pan, folding it to fit. Brush some of the butter on the filo with a pastry brush. Layer a second and a third sheet of filo on top, folding them to fit and brushing each one with butter. Spread the chocolate filling on the filo, distributing it evenly. Layer 2 or 3 more folded, buttered sheets of filo over the filling. Spread the crème de menthe over the filo. Top with 2 or 3 sheets of folded, buttered filo. Before baking, sprinkle a few drops of water over the top and around the edges of the filo to prevent it from curling.

Bake at 350° for 40 to 50 minutes, or until the filo is crisp and golden brown. Cool on a wire rack while making the glaze.

Glaze
Melt the butter over low heat in a small saucepan. Stir in the cocoa and powdered sugar and mix thoroughly. Continue stirring until hot and bubbly. Drizzle the chocolate over the filo. Serve cold.

COCONUT-CHOCOLATE JOY

Makes 12 3-inch servings

16 ounces cream cheese, at room
    temperature
1½ cups coconut, grated
½ cup sour cream
½ cup sugar
2 egg yolks
2 teaspoons almond extract
2 cups semisweet chocolate chips
½ cup almonds, sliced or coarsely
    chopped
1 pound filo leaves, thawed and
    covered with a damp
    kitchen towel
1 cup butter, clarified and melted

Topping

⅓ cup milk chocolate chips
1 tablespoon sour cream
2 tablespoons almonds, sliced or
    coarsely chopped
    (optional)
2 tablespoons coconut, grated
    (optional)

Butter a 7 × 11-inch pan; set aside. Preheat oven to 350°.

In a large mixing bowl combine the cream cheese, coconut, sour cream, and sugar. Beat thoroughly with a mixer. Add the egg yolks and almond extract and mix thoroughly. Melt the chocolate chips in a double boiler over low heat, stirring until smooth. Stir in the melted chocolate and almonds, mixing well.

Lay 1 sheet of filo on a large plastic cutting board. Brush some of the butter on the filo with a pastry brush. Layer a second and a third sheet, brushing each one with butter. Put 1 cup of the chocolate-coconut mixture in a long, narrow row at the short end of the filo. Roll up jelly roll fashion. Tuck the ends underneath. Place the roll seam side down in the buttered pan. Repeat to form additional rolls until all the mixture is used, placing each roll next to the previous one. Brush tops and ends with the remaining melted butter.

Bake at 350° for 40 to 50 minutes, or until the filo is crisp and golden brown. Cool on a wire rack while making the topping.

Topping

Melt the chocolate chips in a double boiler over low heat, stirring until melted and smooth. Stir the sour cream into the melted chocolate. Drizzle the chocolate over the cooled filo. Sprinkle the almonds and coconut on top. Cut the rolls diagonally and serve cold. Serve with a scoop of ice cream or whipped topping, if desired.

❖❖❖

CARAMEL CUSTARD PUFFS

◆

Makes 6 3-inch servings

2 cups cream (or light cream)	½ cup butter, clarified and melted
2 tablespoons cornstarch	powdered sugar (optional)
⅛ teaspoon salt	
¼ cup butter	***Optional Sauce***
¾ cup dark brown sugar	1 cup cream (or light cream)
½ cup dark corn syrup	1 tablespoon cornstarch
6 egg yolks	¼ cup dark brown sugar
2 teaspoons vanilla extract	¼ cup dark corn syrup
¼ cup praline liqueur	1 tablespoon butter
½ cup pecans, chopped	salt
½ pound filo leaves, thawed and	2 teaspoons vanilla extract
covered with a damp	2 tablespoons praline liqueur
kitchen towel	¼ cup pecans

◆

Butter a 6 × 10-inch pan; set aside. Preheat oven to 350°.

In a double boiler combine cream, cornstarch, and salt. Stir until the cornstarch dissolves. Stir in the butter, brown sugar, and corn syrup. Cook over—not immersed in—boiling water. Continue stirring until the butter melts. In a mixing bowl, beat egg yolks thoroughly; stir in 2 tablespoons of the hot mixture, then mix thoroughly. Stir the yolk mixture into the heated custard. Continue stirring until smooth and partially thickened. Stir in the vanilla extract, liqueur, and pecans. Remove from heat and set aside.

Place 1 sheet of filo in the bottom of the buttered pan, folding it to fit. Brush some of the butter on the filo with a pastry brush. Layer a second and a third sheet of folded, buttered filo on top. Pour the custard evenly on the filo. Top with 2 or 3 folded, buttered sheets of filo. Before baking, sprinkle a few drops of water over the top and around the edges of the filo to prevent it from curling.

Bake at 350° for 40 to 50 minutes, or until the custard is set and the filo is brown and crisp. Cool on a wire rack while making the sauce. Dust with powdered sugar, if desired.

Optional Sauce
In a saucepan combine the cream, cornstarch, brown sugar, corn syrup, butter, and salt. Stir until the cornstarch dissolves. Continue to stir over low heat until the butter melts and the mixture is smooth and slightly thickened. Turn the heat off and stir in the vanilla extract, liqueur, and pecans. Pour sauce over individual servings. Serve warm or cold.

APRICOT AND RAISIN-WALNUT ROLL

Makes 8 to 10 2-inch servings

2	cups apricots, peeled and sliced	1	cup butter, clarified and melted
1	cup raisins	1½	cups bread crumbs, toasted
1	cup walnuts, chopped		powdered sugar (optional)
¾	cup brown sugar, packed		
3	egg yolks, well beaten		***Apricot Glaze***
1	teaspoon cinnamon	½	cup apricot preserves
¼	teaspoon cloves	1	tablespoon lemon juice
¼	teaspoon lemon zest	2	teaspoons cornstarch
1	pound filo leaves, thawed and covered with a damp kitchen towel	2	tablespoons walnuts, ground

Butter a 9 × 13-inch pan; set aside. Preheat oven to 350°.

In a large bowl combine the apricots, raisins, walnuts, and brown sugar; mix thoroughly. Stir in the egg yolks, cinnamon, cloves, and lemon zest and mix well. Set aside.

Lay 1 sheet of filo on a large plastic cutting board. Brush some of the butter on the filo with a pastry brush. Layer a second and a third sheet of filo on top, brushing each one with butter. Sprinkle about ¾ cup of the bread crumbs over the filo. Put 1 cup of the filling in a long, narrow row at the short end of the filo. Roll up jelly roll fashion. Tuck the ends underneath. Place the roll seam side down in the buttered pan. Repeat to form additional rolls until all the filling is used, placing each roll next to the previous one. Brush tops and ends with the remaining melted butter.

Bake at 350° for 40 to 50 minutes, or until the filo is crisp and golden brown. Cool on a wire rack. Dust with powdered sugar, if desired, or top with the glaze.

Glaze

Combine the apricot preserves and lemon juice in a small saucepan. Stir in the cornstarch and mix thoroughly. Stir while cooking over low heat until smooth and slightly thickened. Spread the hot glaze over the warm filo. Sprinkle the nuts over the top. Cut the rolls diagonally before serving. Serve warm. Top with whipped cream or ice cream, if desired.

APPLE-RASPBERRY STRUDEL

Makes 6 to 8 2-inch servings

3   cups apples, peeled and sliced
1   cup raspberries
½   cup almonds, chopped
2   teaspoons almond extract
½   cup sugar
1   teaspoon cinnamon
1   teaspoon lemon zest, grated
½   pound filo leaves, thawed and
      covered with a damp
      kitchen towel
½   cup butter, clarified and melted

1½ cup bread crumbs, toasted
      powdered sugar (optional)

Glaze

1   cup raspberry jam
1   tablespoon lemon juice
1   tablespoon cornstarch
2   tablespoons butter
1   teaspoon almond extract
¼   cup almonds, chopped

Butter a 6 × 10-inch pan; set aside. Preheat oven to 350°.

In a medium bowl combine the apples, raspberries, and almonds and mix thoroughly. Stir in the almond extract. In a small bowl combine the sugar, cinnamon, and lemon zest; add to the apple mixture and stir well. Set aside.

Place 1 sheet of filo in the bottom of the buttered pan, folding it to fit. Brush some of the butter on the filo with a pastry brush. Layer a second and a third sheet of filo on top, folding them to fit and brushing each one with butter. Sprinkle the bread crumbs over the filo. Spread the apple-raspberry mixture over the filo. Top with 2 or 3 sheets of folded, buttered filo. Before baking, sprinkle a few drops of water over the top and around the edges of the filo to prevent it from curling.

Bake at 350° for 40 to 50 minutes, or until the filo is crisp and golden brown. Cool on a wire rack and dust with powdered sugar, if desired, or top with the glaze, spreading it on before the filo has cooled completely.

Glaze
In a small saucepan, combine the raspberry jam, lemon juice, and cornstarch. Stir until the cornstarch dissolves. Stir in the butter. Continue stirring over low heat until hot and bubbly. Stir in the almond extract and almonds. Spread the hot glaze on the warm filo. Serve warm or cold. Serve with whipped cream or ice cream, if desired.

FILO-WRAPPED BANANAS FOSTER

Makes 10 2-inch servings

2	cups cream (or light cream)	½ cup butter, clarified and melted
¼	cup cornstarch	5 medium bananas, sliced
1	teaspoon cinnamon	
⅛	teaspoon salt	***Glaze***
2	tablespoons butter	2 tablespoons butter
¾	cup dark brown sugar	¾ cup powdered sugar
6	egg yolks	1 teaspoon rum flavoring
2	teaspoons vanilla extract	
1	tablespoon rum flavoring	
½	pound filo leaves, thawed and covered with a damp kitchen towel	

Butter a 7 × 11-inch pan; set aside. Preheat oven to 350°.

In a double boiler, combine the cream, cornstarch, cinnamon, and salt. Stir until the cornstarch dissolves. Stir in the butter and sugar. Cook over—not immersed in—boiling water. Continue stirring until the butter melts. In a mixing bowl, beat egg yolks thoroughly; stir in 2 tablespoons of the hot mixture and mix well. Stir the yolk mixture into the heated custard. Continue stirring, until smooth and partially thickened. Stir in the vanilla extract and rum flavoring. Remove from heat and set aside.

Place 1 sheet of filo in the bottom of the buttered pan, folding it to fit. Brush some of the butter on the filo with a pastry brush. Layer a second and a third sheet of folded, buttered filo on top. Arrange the bananas on top of the filo. Pour the custard over the bananas. Top with 3 or 4 folded, buttered sheets of filo. Before baking, sprinkle a few drops of water over the top and around the edges of the filo to prevent it from curling.

Bake at 350° for 40 to 50 minutes, or until the custard is set and the filo is golden brown and crisp. Cool on a wire rack while making the glaze.

Glaze
Melt the butter over low heat in a small saucepan. Stir in the powdered sugar and continue stirring until hot and bubbly. Stir in the rum flavoring, and drizzle the glaze over the warm filo. Serve warm or cold.

PINA COLADA TREATS

◆

Makes 9 3-inch servings

2 cups cream (or light cream)	½ pound filo leaves, thawed and
1 cup cream of coconut	covered with a damp
¼ cup butter	kitchen towel
½ cup sugar	½ cup butter, clarified and melted
6 egg yolks	
1 teaspoon vanilla extract	*Glaze*
1 teaspoon almond extract	1 tablespoon butter
1 teaspoon rum flavoring	2 tablespoons milk
1 cup coconut, grated	½ cup powdered sugar
¾ cup pineapple tidbits, well	¼ cup coconut, grated
drained	½ cup maraschino cherry halves

◆

Butter a 7 × 11-inch pan; set aside. Preheat oven to 350°.

In a double boiler, combine the cream and cream of coconut. Stir in the butter and sugar. Cook over—not immersed in—boiling water. Continue stirring until the butter melts. In a mixing bowl, beat egg yolks thoroughly; stir in two tablespoons of the hot mixture, then mix thoroughly. Stir the yolk mixture into the heated custard. Continue stirring, until partially thickened. Stir in the vanilla extract, almond extract, and rum flavoring. Stir in the coconut and pineapple. Remove from heat and set aside.

Place 1 sheet of filo in the bottom of the buttered pan, folding it to fit. Brush some of the butter on the filo with a pastry brush. Layer a second and a third sheet of filo on top, folding them to fit the pan and brushing each one with butter. Pour the custard on the filo, spreading it out evenly. Top with 2 to 3 folded, buttered sheets of filo. Before baking, sprinkle a few drops of water over the top and around the edges of the filo to prevent it from curling.

Bake at 350° for 40 to 50 minutes, or until the custard is set and the filo is golden brown and crisp. Cool on a wire rack while making the glaze.

Glaze
Melt the butter over low heat in a small saucepan. Stir in the milk and powdered sugar. Continue stirring until hot and bubbly. Stir in the coconut. Spread the glaze over the filo. Decorate with the cherries. Serve warm or cold.

MINI TURTLES

Makes 8 to 10 2-inch servings

8   ounces cream cheese, at room
    temperature
¼   cup dark brown sugar
2   tablespoons (dark) corn syrup
1   teaspoon vanilla extract
2   teaspoons cocoa powder
1½ ounces praline liqueur
2   teaspoons cornstarch
3   egg yolks
½   pound filo leaves, thawed and
    covered with a damp
    kitchen towel
½   cup butter, clarified and melted

Topping

2   tablespoons sour cream, divided
⅓   cup milk chocolate chips
4   pieces of caramel candy,
    individually wrapped
¼   cup pecans, chopped

Butter a 6 × 10-inch pan; set aside. Preheat oven to 350°.

In a medium bowl beat the cream cheese, brown sugar, and corn syrup with an electric mixer. Stir in the vanilla extract, cocoa, praline liqueur, and cornstarch. Add egg yolks, and mix thoroughly. Set aside.

Fold 1 sheet of filo in half, lengthwise, to form a rectangle. Brush some of the butter on the filo with a pastry brush. Spoon about ¾ cup of the filling in a narrow row, down the long side of the filo. Roll up jelly roll fashion. Tuck the ends underneath. Place the roll seam side down in the buttered pan. Repeat to form additional rolls until all the filling is used, placing each roll next to the previous one. Brush tops and ends with the remaining melted butter.

Bake at 350° for 40 to 50 minutes, or until the filo is crisp and golden brown. Cool on a wire rack while making the topping.

Topping

Combine 1 tablespoon of the sour cream and chocolate chips in a small glass dish and microwave on high for 45 seconds. Stir, and repeat, if necessary, until smooth and melted. (Or, melt in a double boiler, over low heat, on the stove.) Drizzle the chocolate over the filo. Put the rest of the sour cream in a small glass dish. Unwrap the caramel candy and add it to the sour cream. Microwave on medium for 1 minute. Stir and repeat, if necessary, until smooth and melted. Drizzle over the chocolate. Sprinkle the pecans on top. Cut diagonally and serve cold.

COCONUT CUSTARD PUFFS

◆

Makes 6 3-inch servings

2   cups cream (or light cream)
1   cup cream of coconut*
¼   cup butter
¼   cup sugar
6   egg yolks
2   teaspoons vanilla extract
1   teaspoon almond extract
2   cups coconut, grated
½   pound filo leaves, thawed and
        covered with a damp
        kitchen towel
½   cup butter, clarified and melted

Glaze
2   tablespoons butter
2   tablespoons milk
¾   cup powdered sugar
¼   cup coconut, grated

◆

Butter a 7 × 11-inch pan; set aside. Preheat oven to 350°.

In a double boiler combine the cream and cream of coconut. Stir in the butter and sugar. Cook over—not immersed in—boiling water. Continue stirring until the butter melts. In a mixing bowl, beat egg yolks thoroughly; stir in two tablespoons of the hot mixture and mix thoroughly. Stir the yolk mixture into the heated custard. Continue stirring, until partially thickened. Stir in the vanilla extract and almond extract, and coconut. Remove from heat and set aside.

Place 1 sheet of filo in the bottom of the buttered pan, folding it to fit. Brush some of the butter on the filo with a pastry brush. Layer a second and a third sheet of filo on top, folding them to fit and brushing each one with butter. Pour the custard on the filo, spreading it evenly. Top with 2 to 3 folded, buttered sheets of filo. Before baking, sprinkle a few drops of water over the top and around the edges of the filo to prevent it from curling.

Bake at 350° for 40 to 50 minutes, or until the custard is set and the filo is golden brown and crisp. Cool on a wire rack while making the glaze.

Glaze
Melt the butter over low heat in a small saucepan. Stir in the milk and powdered sugar and continue stirring until hot and bubbly. Stir in the coconut. Spread the glaze over the filo. Serve warm or cold.

*Cream of coconut is found in the beverage section at your supermarket.

❖❖❖

CHOCOLATE-NUT FINGERS

◆

Makes 20 to 25 2-inch servings

Syrup
1½ cups sugar
1½ cups water
2   tablespoons lemon juice
½   cup honey

Filling
2   cups walnuts, ground
1   cup almonds, ground
2   cups coconut, finely grated
¾   cup sugar

¼   cup cocoa powder
1½ teaspoons cinnamon

1   pound filo leaves, thawed and
        covered with a damp
        kitchen towel
1   cup butter, clarified and melted

Glaze
1   ounce milk chocolate chips
1   tablespoon sour cream

◆

Butter a 7 × 11-inch pan; set aside. Preheat oven to 350°.

Syrup
In a large, heavy saucepan combine the sugar, water, and lemon juice. Stir over low heat until the sugar dissolves. Bring the syrup to a boil, then turn the heat down and simmer for 20 to 25 minutes. Stir in the honey. Let cool while making the filling.

Filling
In a large bowl combine the walnuts, almonds, and coconut. In a small bowl, combine the sugar, cocoa, and cinnamon; pour into the nut mixture and mix thoroughly.

Lay 1 sheet of filo on a large plastic cutting board. Brush some of the butter on the filo with a pastry brush. Layer a second and a third sheet of buttered filo on top of the first. Put 1 cup of the filling in a long, narrow row along the short end of the filo. Roll up jelly roll fashion. Tuck the ends underneath. Place the roll seam side down in the buttered pan. Repeat to form additional rolls until all the filling is used, placing each roll next to the previous one. Butter the tops and sides of the rolls with the remaining butter. Cut the top layers of the filo diagonally before baking.

Bake at 350° for 40 to 50 minutes, or until the filo is crisp and golden brown. Pour the cool syrup over the hot filo. Cool on a wire rack while making the glaze.

Glaze
Melt the chocolate chips in a double boiler over low heat, stirring until smooth. Stir the sour cream into the melted chocolate. Drizzle the chocolate glaze over the

filo. After cooling, finish cutting into diamond shapes, by cutting through the bottom layers of the filo. Cover before storing.

Note: This dessert is better if made a day ahead.

COFFEE AND CREAM SQUARES

◆

Makes 12 2-inch servings

24 ounces cream cheese, at room temperature
½ cup coffee-flavored liqueur
½ cup sugar
2 teaspoons vanilla extract
4 teaspoons instant coffee, dissolved in 1 tablespoon hot water
3 egg yolks
½ pound filo leaves, thawed and covered with a damp kitchen towel

½ cup butter, clarified and melted

Glaze
2 tablespoons butter, melted
¾ cup powdered sugar
1 teaspoon instant coffee, dissolved in 1 teaspoon hot water
1 tablespoon coffee-flavored liqueur

◆

Butter a 7 × 11-inch pan; set aside. Preheat oven to 350°.

In a large mixing bowl combine the cream cheese, liqueur, sugar, vanilla extract, dissolved coffee, and egg yolks. Beat with a mixer until creamy. Set aside.

Place 1 sheet of filo in the bottom of the buttered pan, folding it to fit. Brush some of the butter on the filo with a pastry brush. Layer a second and a third sheet of filo on top, folding them to fit and brushing each one with butter. Put the filling on the buttered filo, spreading it out evenly. Top with 2 or 3 folded, buttered sheets of filo. Before baking, sprinkle a few drops of water over the top and around the edges of the filo to prevent it from curling.

Bake at 350° for 40 to 50 minutes, or until the filling is set and the filo is crisp and golden brown. Cool on a wire rack while making the glaze.

Glaze
Melt the butter over low heat in a small saucepan. Stir in the powdered sugar, dissolved coffee, and liqueur. Mix thoroughly and stir until hot and bubbly. Drizzle the glaze over the warm filo creating a design. Serve warm or cold.

BLUEBERRY-PECAN DELIGHT

Makes 16 to 18 2-inch servings

2 pints blueberries	1 cup butter, clarified and melted
1 cup pecans (or other nuts), chopped	2 cup bread crumbs, divided
¾ cup sugar	***Glaze***
1 teaspoon cinnamon	2 tablespoons butter
2 teaspoons lemon peel, grated	¾ cup powdered sugar
2 teaspoons vanilla extract	¼ cup blueberry preserves
1 teaspoon lemon extract	¼ cup nuts, chopped
3 egg yolks, beaten	
1 pound filo leaves, thawed and covered with a damp kitchen towel	

Butter a 9 × 13-inch pan; set aside. Preheat oven to 350°.

In a large bowl combine the blueberries, nuts, sugar, cinnamon, lemon zest, vanilla extract, and lemon extract. Mix thoroughly. Stir in the beaten egg yolks and mix thoroughly.

Lay 1 sheet of filo on a large plastic cutting board. Brush some of the butter on the filo with a pastry brush. Layer a second and a third sheet of filo on top, brushing each one with butter. Sprinkle ½ cup of the bread crumbs over the filo. Put 1 cup of the blueberry mixture in a long narrow row at the short end of the filo. Roll up jelly roll fashion. Tuck the ends underneath. Place the roll seam side down in the buttered pan. Repeat to form additional rolls until all the filling is used, placing each roll next to the previous one. Brush the tops and ends with the remaining melted butter.

Bake at 350° for 40 to 50 minutes, or until the filo is crisp and golden brown. Cool on a wire rack while making the glaze.

Glaze
Melt the butter over low heat in a small saucepan. Stir in the powdered sugar and preserves and continue stirring until hot and bubbly. Drizzle the glaze over the filo and sprinkle the nuts on top. Cut the rolls diagonally before serving. Serve hot or cold. Serve with whipped cream or ice cream, if desired.

CHOCOLATE BANANA DREAM

◆

Makes 8 3-inch servings

16 ounces cream cheese, at room temperature
½ cup sugar
2 teaspoons banana extract
4 egg yolks
2 medium bananas, peeled and mashed with a fork
1 cup chocolate cookies (about 15), crushed, divided

1 pound filo leaves, thawed and covered with a damp kitchen towel
1 cup butter, clarified and melted

Glaze
2 tablespoons butter
2 teaspoons cocoa powder
¾ cup powdered sugar

◆

Butter an 8 × 8-inch pan; set aside. Preheat oven to 350°.

In a medium bowl combine the cream cheese, sugar, banana extract, and egg yolks. Beat with an electric mixer until thoroughly blended. Stir the mashed bananas in by hand and mix thoroughly. Set aside. Crush the cookies in a food processor, or put them in a plastic bag and crush them with a rolling pin, and set aside.

Place 1 sheet of filo in the bottom of the buttered pan, folding it to fit. Brush some of the butter on the filo with a pastry brush. Layer a second and a third sheet of folded, buttered filo on top. Sprinkle half of the cookie crumbs over the buttered filo. Spread half the banana filling on the cookie crumbs, distributing it evenly. Top with 2 or 3 more folded, buttered sheets of filo. Sprinkle all but 2 tablespoons of the remaining cookie crumbs over the filo, spread the other half of the banana filling over the cookie crumbs. Top with 2 or 3 sheets of folded, buttered filo. Sprinkle the 2 remaining tablespoons of cookie crumbs over the top layer of the filo. Before baking, sprinkle a few drops of water over the top and around the edges of the filo to prevent it from curling.

Bake at 350° for 40 to 50 minutes, or until the filo is crisp and golden brown. Cool on a wire rack while making the glaze.

Glaze
In a small saucepan, melt the butter over low heat. Stir in the cocoa powder and powdered sugar, continuing to stir until hot, bubbly, and well blended. Drizzle the chocolate glaze over the warm filo forming a design. Serve warm or cold.

THREE-CHOCOLATE BAKLAVA

◆

Makes 25 2-inch servings

Syrup
1½ cups sugar
¾ cup water
2 tablespoons lemon juice
¾ cup honey
2 ounces chocolate liqueur

Filling
2 cups walnuts, ground
2 cups almonds, ground
2 cups coconut, grated

3 tablespoons sugar
12 ounces milk chocolate chips

1 pound filo leaves, thawed and
   covered with a damp
   kitchen towel
1 cup butter, clarified and melted

Topping
3 ounces white chocolate
2 tablespoons sour cream

◆

Butter a 9 × 13-inch pan; set aside. Preheat oven to 350°.

Syrup
In a heavy saucepan combine the sugar, water, and lemon juice. Stir over low heat, until the sugar dissolves. Bring the syrup to a boil, then turn the heat down and simmer for 20 to 25 minutes. Stir in the honey and liqueur. Let cool while making the filling.

Filling
In a medium bowl combine the walnuts, almonds, coconut, and sugar and mix thoroughly. Melt the chocolate chips in a double boiler over low heat, stirring until smooth. Stir the melted chocolate into the walnut mixture and mix thoroughly. Set aside.

Lay 1 sheet of filo on a large plastic cutting board. Brush some of the butter on the filo with a pastry brush. Layer a second and a third sheet of filo on top, brushing each with butter. Put about ¾ cup of filling in a long row at the narrow end of the filo. Roll up jelly roll fashion. Tuck the ends underneath. Place the roll seam side down in the buttered pan. Repeat to form additional rolls until all the filling has been used, placing each roll next to the previous one. Brush tops and ends with the remaining melted butter. Cut the top layers of filo diagonally before baking.

Bake at 350° for 40 to 50 minutes, or until the filo is crisp and golden brown. Pour the cool syrup on the hot baklava.

After the baklava has cooled, melt the chocolate in a double boiler over low heat, stirring until smooth. Stir the sour cream into the melted chocolate.

Drizzle the chocolate mixture over the baklava. When the filo is cool, complete the previously begun diagonal cuts by cutting through the bottom layers. Rotate the pan one-quarter of a turn and cut straight rows, making diamond-shaped servings.

SOUTHERN CHESS CUSTARD PUFFS

◆

Makes 6 3-inch servings

½ cup butter, melted
1 cup sugar
4 eggs
2 egg yolks
1 teaspoon almond extract
1 teaspoon lemon extract
2 tablespoons white vinegar
½ pound filo leaves, thawed and covered with a damp kitchen towel

½ cup butter, clarified and melted

Glaze
¾ cup powdered sugar
2 tablespoons amaretto
¼ cup almonds, chopped

◆

Butter a 6 × 10-inch pan; set aside. Preheat oven to 325°.

In a large mixing bowl combine the melted butter, sugar, eggs, and egg yolks, beating with a mixer until smooth and thoroughly mixed. Stir in the almond extract, lemon extract, and vinegar. Set aside.

Place 1 sheet of filo in the bottom of the buttered pan, folding it to fit. Brush some of the butter on the filo with a pastry brush. Layer a second and a third sheet of filo on top, folding them to fit and brushing each one with butter. Pour the custard evenly over the filo. Top with 2 to 3 folded, buttered sheets of filo. Before baking, sprinkle a few drops of water over the top and around the edges of the filo to prevent it from curling.

Bake at 325° for 50 to 60 minutes, or until the custard is set and the filo is golden brown and crisp. Cool on a wire rack while making the glaze.

Glaze
Combine the powdered sugar and amaretto in a small saucepan. Stir over low heat, until smooth, hot, and bubbly. Drizzle the glaze over the filo. Sprinkle the almonds over the top. Serve hot or cold.

Note: This dessert is very rich and should be served in small pieces.

NUTTY COCONUT-FRUIT ROLL UPS

◆

Makes 20 2-inch servings

Syrup

1　cup sugar
1½　cups water
2　tablespoons lemon juice
¾　cup honey
1　teaspoon orange extract
1　teaspoon vanilla extract
2　teaspoons almond extract
¼　cup amaretto

Filling

24　ounces prunes, pitted and finely chopped

½　pound dried apricots, finely chopped
1　cup almonds, ground
½　cup walnuts, ground
12　ounces nut filling, for cakes, pastries, and desserts*
2　cups coconut, grated
2　teaspoons cinnamon

1　pound filo leaves, thawed and covered with a damp kitchen towel
1　cup butter, clarified and melted

◆

Butter a 9 × 13-inch pan; set aside. Preheat oven to 350°.

Syrup

In a medium, heavy saucepan combine the sugar, water, and lemon juice. Stir over low heat until the sugar dissolves. Bring to a boil, then turn the heat down and simmer for 20 minutes. Stir in the honey, orange extract, vanilla extract, almond extract, and amaretto. Let cool while making the filling.

Filling

In a large bowl combine the prunes, apricots, almonds, and walnuts. Stir in the nut filling, coconut, and cinnamon; mix thoroughly. Set aside.

Lay 1 sheet of filo on a large plastic cutting board. Brush some of the butter on the filo with a pastry brush. Layer a second and a third sheet of filo on top, brushing each one with butter. Put 1 cup of the prune mixture in a long narrow row across the short end of the filo. Roll up jelly roll fashion. Tuck the ends underneath. Place the roll seam side down in the buttered pan. Repeat to form additional rolls until all the filling is used, placing each roll next to the previous one. Brush the tops with the remaining melted butter. Cut the top layers of the filo diagonally before baking.

*Nut filling is made with various nuts and has a liqueurlike taste. It can be found in the specialty food section of your supermarket.

Bake at 350° for 40 to 50 minutes, or until the filo is crisp and golden brown. Pour the cool syrup over the hot filo. Cut the rolls diagonally before serving. When cooled, cover before storing.

Note: This dessert is better if made a day ahead.

SUNSET ORANGE COOLER

◆

Makes 6 3-inch servings

16 ounces cream cheese, at room temperature
½ cup sugar
¼ cup frozen orange juice concentrate, thawed
2 teaspoons orange extract
2 egg yolks
2 drops orange food coloring
½ pound filo leaves, thawed and covered with a damp kitchen towel

½ cup butter, clarified and melted

Glaze
2 teaspoons cornstarch
2 ounces frozen orange juice concentrate, thawed
¼ cup orange marmalade

◆

Butter a 6 × 10-inch pan; set aside. Preheat oven to 350°.

In a medium bowl, combine the cream cheese, sugar, orange juice, and orange extract. Beat with a mixer until creamy. Stir in the egg yolks and food coloring and mix thoroughly. Set aside.

Place 1 sheet of filo in the bottom of the buttered pan, folding it to fit. Brush some of the butter on the filo with a pastry brush. Layer a second and a third sheet of filo on top, folding them to fit the pan and brushing each one with butter. Spoon the filling onto the filo, spreading it out evenly. Top with 2 or 3 sheets of folded, buttered filo. Before baking, sprinkle a few drops of water over the top and around the edges of the filo to prevent it from curling.

Bake at 350° for 40 to 50 minutes, or until the filo is golden brown and crisp. Cool on a wire rack while making the glaze.

Glaze
In a saucepan dissolve the cornstarch in the orange juice. Stir in the marmalade and mix thoroughly. Stir over low heat until thickened. Spread the glaze over the warm filo. Serve cold.

TOASTED ALMONDS AND AMARETTO STRUDEL

Makes 9 3-inch servings

16 ounces cream cheese, at room temperature
8 ounces almond paste
½ cup sugar
¼ cup amaretto
¼ cup sour cream
2 teaspoons almond extract
2 teaspoons vanilla extract
2 teaspoons orange extract
2 egg yolks
½ cup almonds, toasted and chopped or sliced

½ pound filo leaves, thawed and covered with a damp kitchen towel
½ cup butter, clarified and melted

Glaze

1 tablespoon butter
¼ cup orange marmalade
½ cup powdered sugar
¼ cup almonds, chopped or sliced

Butter a 7 × 11-inch pan; set aside. Preheat oven to 350°.

In a large bowl combine the cream cheese, almond paste, sugar, amaretto, and sour cream. Beat with an electric mixer until creamy. Stir in the almond, vanilla, and orange extracts. Add the egg yolks and almonds and beat until thoroughly blended. Set aside.

Place 1 sheet of filo in the bottom of the buttered pan, folding it to fit. Brush some of the butter on the filo with a pastry brush. Layer a second and a third sheet of filo on top, folding them to fit and brushing each one with butter. Spread the amaretto mixture on the buttered filo. Top with 2 or 3 sheets of folded, buttered filo. Before baking, sprinkle a few drops of water over the top and around the edges of the filo, to prevent it from curling.

Bake at 350° for 40 to 50 minutes, or until top is crisp and golden brown. Cool on a wire rack while making the glaze.

Glaze

In a saucepan melt the butter over low heat. Add the orange marmalade and powdered sugar, continuing to stir until hot and bubbly. Drizzle the glaze over the warm filo and sprinkle the almonds on top. Serve warm or cold.

CHOCOLATE PRALINE CUSTARD PUFFS

Makes 6 3-inch servings

2	cups cream (or light cream)	½	pound filo leaves, thawed and covered with a damp kitchen towel
⅛	teaspoon salt		
¼	cup butter		
1	cup dark brown sugar	½	cup butter, clarified and melted
6	egg yolks		
8	ounces semisweet chocolate chips		**Glaze**
2	teaspoons vanilla extract	2	ounces semisweet chocolate chips
¼	cup praline liqueur	2	tablespoons sour cream
½	cup pecans, chopped	¼	cup pecans

◆

Butter a 7 × 11-inch pan; set aside. Preheat oven to 350°.

In a double boiler combine the cream, salt, butter, and brown sugar. Cook over—not immersed in—boiling water. Continue stirring until the butter melts. In a mixing bowl, beat egg yolks thoroughly; stir in 2 tablespoons of the hot mixture and mix thoroughly. Stir the yolk mixture into the heated custard. Stir in the chocolate chips. Continue stirring until the chocolate melts and the mixture is partially thickened. Add the vanilla extract, liqueur, and pecans. Remove from heat and set aside.

Place 1 sheet of filo in the bottom of the buttered pan, folding it to fit. Brush some of the butter on the filo with a pastry brush. Layer a second and a third sheet of folded, buttered filo on top. Pour the custard on the filo and spread evenly. Top with 2 or 3 sheets of folded, buttered filo. Before baking, sprinkle a few drops of water over the top and around the edges of the filo to prevent it from curling.

Bake at 350° for 40 to 50 minutes, or until the custard is set and the filo is golden brown and crisp. Cool on a wire rack while making the glaze.

Glaze

In a small saucepan combine the chocolate chips and sour cream. Stir continuously over low heat, until the chocolate melts. Drizzle the chocolate mixture over the filo. Sprinkle the pecans on top. Serve warm or cold.

BANANA CREAM CUSTARD PUFFS

Makes 10 2-inch servings

2 cups cream (or light cream)	½ cup butter, clarified and melted
¼ cup cornstarch	5 medium bananas, sliced
⅛ teaspoon salt	
¼ cup butter	**Glaze**
¾ cup sugar	2 tablespoons butter
6 egg yolks	¾ cup powdered sugar
2 teaspoons vanilla extract	1 tablespoon banana schnapps
¼ cup banana schnapps	
½ pound filo leaves, thawed and covered with a damp kitchen towel	

Butter a 7 × 11-inch pan; set aside. Preheat oven to 350°.

In a double boiler, combine the cream, cornstarch, and salt. Stir until the cornstarch dissolves. Stir in the butter and sugar. Cook over—not immersed in—boiling water. Continue stirring until the butter melts. In a mixing bowl, beat egg yolks well; stir in two tablespoons of the hot mixture and mix thoroughly. Stir the yolk mixture into the heated custard. Continue stirring, until smooth and partially thickened. Stir in the vanilla extract and banana schnapps. Remove from heat and set aside.

Place 1 sheet of filo in the bottom of the buttered pan, folding it to fit. Brush some of the butter on the filo with a pastry brush. Layer a second and a third sheet of filo on top, folding them to fit and brushing each one with butter. Arrange the bananas on top of the filo. Pour the custard over the bananas. Top with 2 or 3 folded, buttered sheets of filo. Before baking, sprinkle a few drops of water over the top and around the edges of the filo to prevent it from curling.

Bake at 350° for 40 to 50 minutes, or until the custard is set and the filo is golden brown and crisp. Cool on a wire rack while making the glaze.

Glaze
Melt the butter over low heat in a small saucepan. Stir in the powdered sugar and schnapps and continue stirring until hot and bubbly. Spread the glaze over the filo. Serve warm or cold.

SHOOFLY PIE

◆

Makes 6 3-inch servings

2 cups cream (or light cream)	
¼ cup cornstarch	
⅛ teaspoon salt	
¼ cup butter	
½ cup dark brown sugar	
½ cup unsulphured molasses	
6 egg yolks	
2 teaspoons vanilla extract	
1 cup walnuts, chopped	
½ pound filo leaves, thawed and covered with a damp kitchen towel	
½ cup butter, clarified and melted	

Sauce

1 cup cream or light cream
1 tablespoon cornstarch
3 tablespoons brown sugar
¼ cup unsulphured molasses
   salt
2 teaspoons vanilla extract

◆

Butter a 6 × 10-inch pan; set aside. Preheat oven to 350°.

In a double boiler combine the cream, cornstarch, and salt. Stir until the cornstarch dissolves. Stir in the butter, brown sugar, and molasses. Cook over—not immersed in—boiling water. Continue stirring until the butter melts and the sugar dissolves. In a mixing bowl, beat egg yolks thoroughly; stir in two tablespoons of the hot mixture, then mix thoroughly. Stir the yolk mixture into the heated custard. Continue stirring, until smooth and partially thickened. Stir in the vanilla extract and walnuts. Remove from heat and set aside.

Place 1 sheet of filo in the bottom of the buttered pan, folding it to fit. Brush some of the butter on the filo with a pastry brush. Layer a second and a third sheet of folded, buttered filo on top. Pour the custard evenly on the filo. Top with 2 to 3 folded, buttered sheets of filo. Before baking, sprinkle a few drops of water over the top and around the edges of the filo to prevent it from curling.

Bake at 350° for 40 to 50 minutes, or until the custard is set and the filo is golden brown and crisp. Cool on a wire rack while making the sauce.

Sauce

In a saucepan combine the cream and cornstarch. Stir until the cornstarch dissolves. Stir in the brown sugar, molasses, and salt. Stir continuously while cooking over low heat until the sugar dissolves and the sauce is smooth and slightly thickened. Turn the heat off and stir in the vanilla extract. Pour the sauce over the individual servings. Serve warm or cold.

MOCHA WALNUT CUSTARD PUFFS

Makes 6 3-inch servings

2 cups cream (or light cream)
¼ cup cornstarch
⅛ teaspoon salt
¼ cup butter
1 cup sweetened condensed milk
6 egg yolks
2 teaspoons vanilla extract
2 teaspoons instant coffee, dissolved in 1 tablespoon hot water
¼ cup coffee-flavored liqueur
1 cup walnuts, chopped

4 ounces semisweet chocolate chips
¼ cup sugar
½ pound filo leaves, thawed and covered with a damp kitchen towel
½ cup butter, clarified and melted

Topping

2 ounces milk chocolate chips
2 tablespoons sour cream
1 teaspoon instant coffee, dissolved in 1 teaspoon hot water

Butter a 6 × 10-inch pan; set aside. Preheat oven to 350°.

In a double boiler, combine the cream, cornstarch, and salt. Stir until the cornstarch dissolves. Stir in the butter and condensed milk. Cook over—not immersed in—boiling water. Continue stirring until the butter melts. In a mixing bowl, beat egg yolks thoroughly; stir in 2 tablespoons of the hot mixture, then mix thoroughly. Stir the yolk mixture into the heated custard. Continue stirring until smooth and partially thickened. Stir in the vanilla extract, dissolved coffee, liqueur, and walnuts. Remove from heat, pour half of this mixture into a small bowl, and set aside.

Stir the chocolate chips and sugar into the remaining custard. Stir until the chocolate melts and the sugar dissolves. Set aside.

Place 1 sheet of filo in the bottom of the buttered pan, folding it to fit. Brush some of the butter on the filo with a pastry brush. Layer a second and a third sheet of folded, buttered filo on top. Pour the chocolate custard evenly on the filo. Top with 2 folded, buttered sheets of filo. Pour the remaining custard on and spread evenly. Cover with 2 or 3 folded, buttered sheets of filo. Before baking, sprinkle a few drops of water over the top and around the edges of the filo to prevent it from curling.

Bake at 350° for 40 to 50 minutes, or until the custard is set and the filo is golden brown and crisp. Cool on a wire rack while making the topping.

Topping

In a saucepan combine the chocolate chips, sour cream, and dissolved coffee. Stir over low heat, until chocolate melts and mixture is creamy. Drizzle the topping over the filo. Serve warm or cold.

LIME COOLER

◆

Makes 6 3-inch servings

16	ounces cream cheese, at room temperature	½	cup butter, clarified and melted
½	cup sugar		***Glaze***
2	tablespoons cornstarch	1	tablespoon butter
½	cup frozen limeade concentrate, thawed	½	cup powdered sugar
1	teaspoon lemon extract	1	tablespoon frozen limeade concentrate, thawed
1	teaspoon grated lime zest	1	drop green food coloring
2	egg yolks		lime slices for decoration
2	drops green food coloring		
½	pound filo leaves, thawed and covered with a damp kitchen towel		

◆

Butter a 6 × 10-inch pan; set aside. Preheat oven to 350°.

In a medium bowl put the cream cheese, sugar, cornstarch, limeade, and lemon extract. Using a mixer beat thoroughly. Add the lime zest, egg yolks, and food coloring and mix thoroughly. Set aside.

Place 1 sheet of filo in the bottom of the buttered pan, folding it to fit. Brush some of the butter on the filo with a pastry brush. Layer a second and a third sheet of filo on top, folding each one to fit the pan and brushing each one with butter. Put the cream cheese mixture on the filo, spreading it out evenly. Top with 2 or 3 sheets of folded and buttered filo. Before baking, sprinkle a few drops of water over the top and around the edges of the filo to prevent it from curling.

Bake at 350° for 40 to 50 minutes, or until the filling is set and the filo is golden brown and crisp. Cool on a wire rack while making the glaze.

Glaze

Melt the butter over low heat in a small saucepan. Stir in the powdered sugar, limeade, and food coloring. Continue stirring until smooth, hot and bubbly. Drizzle over the filo. Decorate with lime slices. Serve cold.

MANGO TROPICAL DELIGHT

Makes 6 3-inch servings

1	cup cream (or light cream)	2	tablespoons orange liqueur
¼	cup cornstarch	½	pound filo leaves, thawed and covered with a damp kitchen towel
⅛	teaspoon salt		
2	tablespoon butter		
¾	cup sugar	½	cup butter, clarified and melted
6	egg yolks		
2	teaspoons vanilla extract		**Glaze**
1	teaspoon lemon extract	1	tablespoon butter
1	teaspoon orange extract	1	tablespoon orange liqueur
½	cup crushed pineapple, well drained	¾	cup powdered sugar
		2	tablespoons crushed pineapple, well drained
2	cups mango, mashed		
1	cup coconut, grated	¼	cup coconut, grated

Butter a 7 × 11-inch pan; set aside. Preheat oven to 350°.

In a double boiler, combine the cream, cornstarch, and salt. Stir until the cornstarch dissolves. Stir in the butter and sugar. Cook over—not immersed in—boiling water. Continue stirring until the butter melts. In a mixing bowl, thoroughly beat egg yolks; stir in 2 tablespoons of the hot mixture, then mix thoroughly. Stir the yolk mixture into the heated custard. Continue stirring until smooth and partially thickened. Stir in the vanilla extract, lemon extract, pineapple, mango, coconut, and liqueur. Remove from heat and set aside.

Place 1 sheet of filo in the bottom of the buttered pan, folding it to fit. Brush some of the butter on the filo with a pastry brush. Layer a second and a third sheet of filo on top, folding them to fit the pan and brushing each one with butter. Pour the custard on the filo. Top with 2 or 3 folded, buttered sheets of filo. Before baking, sprinkle a few drops of water over the top and around the edges of the filo to prevent it from curling.

Bake at 350° for 40 to 50 minutes, or until the custard is set and the filo is golden brown and crisp. Cool on a wire rack while making the glaze.

Glaze
Melt the butter over low heat in a small saucepan. Stir in the liqueur, powdered sugar, and pineapple. Continue stirring until hot and bubbly. Stir in the coconut. Spread the glaze over the filo. Serve warm or cold.

GERMAN CHOCOLATE CUSTARD PUFFS

◆

Makes 6 3-inch servings

2　cups cream (or light cream)
2　tablespoons cornstarch
⅛　teaspoon salt
¼　cup butter
4　ounces German sweet chocolate,
　　broken into pieces
¾　cup sugar
6　egg yolks
1　teaspoon vanilla extract
½　pound filo leaves, thawed and
　　covered with a damp
　　kitchen towel
½　cup butter, clarified and melted

Topping

1　tablespoon butter
2　ounces German sweet chocolate
2　tablespoons sour cream
1　tablespoon powdered sugar
¼　cup pecans

◆

Butter a 6 × 10-inch pan; set aside. Preheat oven to 350°.

In a double boiler, combine the cream, cornstarch, and salt. Stir until the cornstarch dissolves. Stir in the butter, chocolate, and sugar. Cook over—not immersed in—boiling water. Continue stirring until the butter and chocolate melt. In a mixing bowl, beat egg yolks thoroughly; stir in two tablespoons of the hot mixture, then mix thoroughly. Stir the yolk mixture into the heated custard. Continue stirring until smooth and partially thickened. Stir in the vanilla extract. Remove from heat and set aside.

Place 1 sheet of filo in the bottom of the buttered pan, folding it to fit. Brush some of the butter on the filo with a pastry brush. Layer a second and a third sheet of filo on top, folding them to fit the pan and brushing each one with butter. Pour the custard evenly over the filo. Top with 2 or 3 folded, buttered sheets of filo. Before baking, sprinkle a few drops of water over the top and around the edges of the filo to prevent it from curling.

Bake at 350° for 40 to 50 minutes, or until the custard is set and the filo is golden brown and crisp. Cool on a wire rack while making the topping.

Topping
Melt the butter and German sweet chocolate over low heat in a small saucepan. Stir in the sour cream, powdered sugar, and nuts, mix thoroughly. Spread the topping over the top of the filo. Serve warm or cold.

COCONUT-ALMOND TART

Makes 15 2-inch servings

16 ounces cream cheese, at room temperature	½ cup butter, clarified and melted
1 tablespoon cornstarch	16 coconut macaroons, crumbled
½ cup sugar	
3 ounces cream of coconut*	***Topping***
4 egg yolks	1 cup whipping cream
1 teaspoon vanilla extract	1 teaspoon vanilla extract
1 teaspoon almond extract	¼ cup powdered sugar
½ cup coconut, flaked or freshly grated	¼ cup coconut, flaked or freshly grated
2 tablespoon almonds, coarsely chopped	2 tablespoons almonds, coarsely chopped
½ pound filo leaves, thawed and covered with a damp kitchen towel	

Butter a 7 × 11-inch pan; set aside. Preheat oven to 350°.

In a medium bowl combine the cream cheese, cornstarch, sugar, cream of coconut, and egg yolks. Mix with an electric mixer until creamy. Stir in the vanilla and almond extracts. Stir in the coconut and almonds, mix thoroughly. Set aside.

Place 1 sheet of filo in the bottom of the buttered pan, folding it to fit. Brush some of the butter on the filo with a pastry brush. Layer a second and a third sheet of filo on top, folding them to fit the pan and brushing each one with butter. Sprinkle half of the crumbled macaroons over the filo. Spread half of the filling over the crumbs. Layer 2 sheets of filo on top of the filling, folding them to fit the pan and brushing each one with butter. Sprinkle the rest of the macaroons over the filo. Spread the rest of the filling over the crumbs. Top with 2 or 3 folded, buttered sheets of filo. Before baking, sprinkle a few drops of water over the top and around the edges of the filo to prevent it from curling.

Bake at 350° for 40 to 50 minutes, or until the filo is crisp and golden brown. Cool on a wire rack while making the topping.

*Cream of coconut can be found in the beverage section of your supermarket.

Topping

In a medium bowl combine the whipping cream, vanilla extract, and powdered sugar. Beat with an electric mixer until stiff. Stir in the coconut. Just before serving, put a couple of tablespoons of whipped cream on each serving and sprinkle a few almonds on top. Serve cold.

DOUBLE CHOCOLATE BROWNIE

◆

Makes 6 3-inch servings

1 cup chocolate chips	½ pound filo leaves, thawed and
5 eggs	covered with a damp kitchen towel
1 cup sugar	½ cup butter, clarified and melted
¼ cup cornstarch	
½ cup butter, melted	***Topping***
2 teaspoons vanilla extract	2 ounces white chocolate
¼ cup chocolate liqueur	2 tablespoons sour cream
1 cup pecans, chopped	¼ cup pecans, chopped

◆

Butter a 6 × 10-inch pan; set aside. Preheat oven to 300°.

Melt the chocolate chips in a double boiler over low heat, stirring until smooth. Put the eggs in a large bowl, and beat well. In a small dish combine the sugar and cornstarch. Stir the sugar into the eggs. Stir in the butter and melted chocolate and mix thoroughly. Stir in the vanilla extract, liqueur, and pecans; mix well and set aside.

Place 1 sheet of filo in the bottom of the buttered pan, folding it to fit. Brush some of the butter on the filo with a pastry brush. Layer a second and a third sheet of folded, buttered filo on top. Pour the mixture on the filo and spread it evenly. Top with 2 or 3 sheets of folded, buttered filo. Before baking, sprinkle a few drops of water over the top and around the edges of the filo to prevent it from curling.

Bake at 300° for 1 hour, or until the brownie filling is done and the filo is crisp and golden brown. Cool on a wire rack while making the topping.

Topping

Melt the chocolate chips in a double boiler over low heat, stirring until smooth. Stir the sour cream into the melted chocolate. Drizzle the topping over the cool filo. Sprinkle the pecans on top.

MACAROON ROLLS

Makes 15 2-inch servings

Syrup

¾ cup sugar
1 cup water
2 tablespoons lemon juice
¾ cup honey
2 teaspoons almond extract
¼ cup amaretto

Filling

4 cups coconut, grated
2 cups almonds, toasted and
    chopped

8 ounces almond paste
½ cup maraschino cherries, chopped
¼ cup rose water*

1 pound filo leaves, thawed and
    covered with a damp
    kitchen towel
1 cup butter, clarified and melted

Butter a 7 × 11-inch pan; set aside. Preheat oven to 350°.

Syrup

In a medium size, heavy saucepan combine the sugar, water, and lemon juice. Stir over low heat until the sugar dissolves. Bring the syrup to a boil, then turn the heat down and simmer for 20 minutes. Stir in the honey, almond extract, and amaretto. Let cool while making the filling.

Filling

In a large bowl combine the coconut, almonds, almond paste, and cherries; mix thoroughly. Stir in the rose water.

Lay 1 sheet of filo on a large plastic cutting board. Brush some of the butter on the filo with a pastry brush. Layer a second and a third sheet of filo on top, brushing each with butter. Put 1 cup of the mixture in a long row across the narrow edge of the filo. Roll up jelly roll fashion. Tuck the ends underneath. Place the roll seam side down in the buttered pan. Repeat to form additional rolls until all the filling has been used, placing each roll next to the previous one. Brush the tops and sides with the remaining melted butter. Cut the top layers of filo diagonally before baking.

Bake at 350° for 40 to 50 minutes, or until the filo is crisp and golden brown. Pour the cool syrup on the hot filo. Complete the previously begun diagonal cuts by

*Rose water is found in Middle Eastern and specialty food stores.

cutting through the bottom layers of the filo. Rotate the pan one-quarter of a turn and cut the filo in straight rows to make diamond-shaped servings. When cool, cover before storing.

NOTE: This dessert is better if made a day ahead.

WHITE CHOCOLATE CUSTARD PIE

Makes 6 3-inch servings

2	cups cream (or light cream)	½	pound filo leaves, thawed and covered with a damp kitchen towel
2	tablespoons cornstarch		
6	ounces white chocolate		
⅛	teaspoon salt	½	cup butter, clarified and melted
¼	cup butter		
½	cup sugar		***Topping***
6	egg yolks	2	ounces white chocolate
2	teaspoons vanilla extract	2	tablespoons sour cream
2	ounces white chocolate liqueur	¼	cup almonds, chopped

Butter a 6 × 10-inch pan; set aside. Preheat oven to 350°.

In a double boiler, combine the cream and cornstarch. Stir until the cornstarch dissolves. Stir in the chocolate, salt, butter, and sugar. Cook over—not immersed in—boiling water. Continue stirring until the chocolate and butter melt. In a mixing bowl, beat egg yolks thoroughly; stir in 2 tablespoons of the hot mixture and mix thoroughly. Stir the yolk mixture into the heated custard. Continue stirring until smooth and partially thickened. Stir in the vanilla extract and liqueur. Remove from heat and set aside.

Place 1 sheet of filo in the bottom of the buttered pan, folding it to fit. Brush some of the butter on the filo with a pastry brush. Layer 2 or 3 folded, buttered sheets of filo. Pour the custard over the filo. Top with 2 or 3 folded, buttered sheets of filo. Before baking, sprinkle a few drops of water over the top and around the edges of the filo to prevent it from curling.

Bake at 350° for 40 to 50 minutes, or until the custard is set and the filo is golden and crisp. Cool on a wire rack while making the topping. Serve warm or cold.

Topping
Melt the chocolate in a small saucepan over low heat. Stir in the sour cream and mix thoroughly. Drizzle the topping over the custard. Sprinkle the almonds on top.

BUTTER PECAN TREATS

Makes 6 3-inch servings

2	cups whole cream (or light cream)	¾	cup pecans, chopped
¼	cup cornstarch	½	pound filo leaves, thawed and covered with a damp kitchen towel
⅛	teaspoon salt		
¼	cup butter	½	cup butter, clarified and melted
½	cup light brown sugar		
⅓	cup dark corn syrup		**Topping**
6	egg yolks	2	tablespoons butter
2	teaspoons vanilla extract	¾	cup powdered sugar
2	tablespoons vanilla-flavored liqueur (such as Tuaca)	2	tablespoons almond brickle chips
		¼	cup pecans

Butter a 6 × 10-inch pan; set aside. Preheat oven to 350°.

In a double boiler, combine the cream, cornstarch, and salt. Stir until the cornstarch dissolves. Stir in the butter, sugar, and corn syrup. Cook over—not immersed in—boiling water. Continue stirring until the butter melts. In a mixing bowl, beat egg yolks well; stir in 2 tablespoons of the hot mixture and mix thoroughly. Stir the egg yolk mixture into the heated custard. Continue stirring, until smooth and partially thickened. Stir in the vanilla extract, liqueur, and pecans. Remove from the heat and set aside.

Place 1 sheet of filo in the bottom of the buttered pan, folding it to fit. Brush some of the butter on the filo with a pastry brush. Layer a second and a third sheet of filo on top, folding them to fit and brushing each one with butter. Pour the custard on the filo. Top with 2 or 3 folded, buttered sheets of filo. Before baking, sprinkle a few drops of water over the top and around the edges of the filo to prevent it from curling.

Bake at 350° for 40 to 50 minutes, or until the custard is set and the filo is golden and crisp. Cool on a wire rack while making the topping.

Topping
Melt the butter over low heat in a small saucepan. Stir in the powdered sugar and continue stirring until hot and bubbly. Stir in the almond brickle chips and pecans. Spread the topping evenly over the warm filo. Serve warm or cold.

VANILLA CREAM EXTRAORDINAIRE

◆

Makes 10 3-inch servings

24 ounces cream cheese, at room
    temperature
½ cup sugar
½ cup honey
2 tablespoons cornstarch
1 tablespoon vanilla extract
1 teaspoon almond extract
¼ cup vanilla-flavored liqueur
    (such as Tuaca)
3 egg yolks
½ pound filo leaves, thawed and
    covered with a damp
    kitchen towel
½ cup butter, clarified and melted

Sauce
1 cup cream or light cream
1 tablespoon cornstarch
2 tablespoons sugar
    salt
¼ cup honey
2 teaspoons vanilla extract
2 tablespoons vanilla-flavored
    liqueur (such as Tuaca)
⅓ cup pecans, chopped

◆

Butter a 7 × 11-inch pan; set aside. Preheat oven to 350°.

In a large mixing bowl, combine the cream cheese, sugar, honey, cornstarch, vanilla extract, almond extract, and vanilla liqueur. Beat with a mixer until creamy. Add the egg yolks and beat until thoroughly mixed. Set aside.

Place 1 sheet of filo in the bottom of the buttered pan, folding it to fit. Brush some of the butter on the filo with a pastry brush. Layer a second and a third sheet of filo on top, folding them to fit and brushing each one with butter. Spread the vanilla mixture on the filo. Top with 2 or 3 folded, buttered sheets of filo. Before baking, sprinkle a few drops of water over the top and around the edges of the filo to prevent it from curling.

Bake at 350° for 40 to 50 minutes, or until the filo is crisp and golden brown. Cool on a wire rack while making the sauce.

Sauce

In a medium saucepan combine the cream and cornstarch, stirring until the cornstarch dissolves. Stir in the sugar, dash of salt, and honey. Continue to stir while cooking over low heat, until the sugar dissolves and the mixture is smooth and slightly thickened. Turn the heat off and stir in the vanilla extract, vanilla liqueur and pecans. Pour the sauce over the filo and serve warm or cold.

LEMON CUSTARD PUFFS

Makes 6 3-inch servings

11 ounces frozen lemonade
concentrate, thawed
¼ cup cornstarch
8 ounces cream cheese, at room
temperature
¼ cup butter
½ cup sugar
6 egg yolks
1 teaspoon lemon extract
1 drop yellow food coloring
½ pound filo leaves, thawed and
covered with a damp kitchen towel
½ cup butter, clarified and melted

Glaze
1 tablespoon butter
½ cup powdered sugar
1 tablespoon frozen lemonade
concentrate, thawed
1 drop yellow food coloring

Butter a 6 × 10-inch pan; set aside. Preheat oven to 350°.

In a double boiler, combine the lemonade and cornstarch. Stir until the
cornstarch dissolves. Stir in the cream cheese and beat until smooth. Cook
over—not immersed in—boiling water. Stir in the butter and sugar. Continue stirring
until the butter melts. In a mixing bowl, beat egg yolks well; stir in two
tablespoons of the hot mixture and mix thoroughly. Stir the yolk mixture into the
heated lemon mixture. Continue stirring until smooth and partially thickened.
Stir in the lemon extract and food coloring. Remove from heat and set aside.

Place 1 sheet of filo in the bottom of the buttered pan, folding it to fit. Brush some
of the butter on the filo with a pastry brush. Layer a second and a third sheet of
filo on top, folding them to fit and brushing each one with butter. Pour the custard
evenly on the filo. Top with 2 to 3 folded, buttered sheets of filo. Before baking,
sprinkle a few drops of water over the top and around the edges of the filo to
prevent it from curling.

Bake at 350° for 40 to 50 minutes, or until the custard is set and the filo is golden
brown and crisp. Cool on a wire rack while making the glaze.

Glaze
Melt the butter over low heat in a small saucepan. Stir in the powdered sugar and
lemonade. Continue stirring until smooth, hot, and bubbly. Stir in the food
coloring. Drizzle the glaze over the filo. Serve warm or cold.

ITALIAN CREAM SQUARES

◆

Makes 6 3-inch servings

1½ pounds ricotta cheese	½ cup golden raisins
8 ounces cream cheese, at room temperature	½ cup mini chocolate chips
1 cup sugar	½ pound filo leaves, thawed and covered with a damp kitchen towel
¼ cup cornstarch	½ cup butter, clarified and melted
¼ cup amaretto	
2 teaspoons almond extract	
2 teaspoons vanilla extract	***Glaze***
2 teaspoons orange extract	1 tablespoon butter
1 teaspoon lemon extract	½ cup powdered sugar
2 teaspoons lemon peel, grated	2 tablespoons amaretto
2 teaspoons orange peel, grated	2 tablespoons almonds, sliced
6 egg yolks	
½ cup almonds, toasted, sliced or chopped	

◆

Butter a 6 × 10-inch pan; set aside. Preheat oven to 325°.

In a large bowl combine the ricotta, cream cheese, sugar, cornstarch, and amaretto. Beat thoroughly with a mixer, until very creamy. Stir in the almond extract, vanilla extract, orange extract, and lemon extract, lemon peel, and orange peel. Add the egg yolks and mix thoroughly. Stir in the almonds, raisins, and chocolate chips. Set aside.

Place 1 sheet of filo in the bottom of the buttered pan, folding it to fit. Brush some of the butter on the filo with a pastry brush. Layer a second and a third sheet of folded, buttered filo. Spread the cheese mixture evenly on the filo. Top with 2 or 3 sheets of folded, buttered filo. Before baking, sprinkle a few drops of water over the top and around the edges of the filo to prevent it from curling.

Bake at 325° for 50 to 60 minutes, or until custard is set and the filo is golden brown and crisp. Cool on a wire rack.

Glaze

Melt the butter over low heat in a small saucepan. Stir in the powdered sugar and amaretto and continue stirring until hot and bubbly. Drizzle the warm glaze over the cooled filo. Decorate with almonds. Serve warm or cold.

POPPY SEED ROLL-UPS

◆

Makes 15 2-inch servings

12 ounces cream cheese, at room temperature	1 pound filo leaves, thawed and covered with a damp kitchen towel
12 ounces poppy seed filling*	1 cup butter, clarified and melted
¼ cup orange liqueur	
⅓ cup sugar	
1 egg	***Glaze***
1 teaspoon butter flavoring	1 tablespoon butter
2 teaspoons orange extract	¼ cup orange marmalade
1 teaspoon vanilla extract	½ cup powdered sugar
1 teaspoon almond extract	¼ cup almonds, sliced or chopped

◆

Butter a 6 × 10-inch pan; set aside. Preheat oven to 350°.

In a large bowl combine the cream cheese, poppy seed filling, orange liqueur, sugar, and egg. Beat with a mixer until thoroughly blended. Stir in the butter flavoring, orange extract, vanilla extract, and almond extract. Set aside.

Lay 1 sheet of filo on a large plastic cutting board. Brush some of the butter on the filo with a pastry brush. Layer a second and a third sheet of filo on top, folding them to fit the pan and brushing each one with butter. Put 1 cup of mixture in a long, narrow row at short end of the filo. Roll up jelly roll fashion. Tuck the ends underneath. Place the roll seam side down in the buttered pan. Repeat to form additional rolls until all the filling is used, placing each roll next to the previous one. Brush the tops and ends with the remaining melted butter.

Bake at 350° for 40 to 50 minutes, or until the filo is golden brown and crisp. Cool on a wire rack while making the glaze.

Glaze
Melt the butter over low heat in a small saucepan. Stir in the marmalade and powdered sugar. Continue stirring until smooth, hot, and bubbly. Drizzle the glaze over the warm filo. Sprinkle the almonds on the top. Cut the rolls diagonally before serving. Serve cold or hot.

*Poppy seed filling can be found in the specialty food section of your supermarket.

PISTACHIO FINGERS

◆

Makes 20 to 25 2-inch servings

Syrup

1½ cups sugar
1 cup water
2 tablespoons lemon juice
½ cup honey

4 tablespoons sugar
1 teaspoon cinnamon
¼ teaspoon nutmeg
¼ teaspoon cloves
¼ cup rose water*

Filling

2 cups walnuts, ground
1 cup pistachios, ground
1 cup almonds, ground
1 cup coconut, grated

1 pound filo leaves, thawed and
  covered with a damp
  kitchen towel
1 cup butter, clarified and melted

◆

Butter a 7 × 11-inch pan; set aside. Preheat oven to 350°.

Syrup

In a large, heavy saucepan combine the sugar, water, and lemon juice. Stir over low heat until the sugar dissolves. Bring the syrup to a boil, then turn the heat down and simmer for 20 to 25 minutes. Stir in the honey. Let cool while making the filling.

Filling

In a large bowl combine the walnuts, pistachios, almonds, and coconut. Mix the sugar, cinnamon, nutmeg, and cloves in a cup. Add the rose water to the mixture in the cup. Pour over the nut mixture and mix thoroughly.

Lay 1 sheet of filo on a large plastic cutting board. Brush some of the butter on the filo with a pastry brush. Layer a second and a third sheet of filo on top, brushing each one with butter. Put 1 cup of the filling in a long, narrow row along the short end of the filo. Roll up jelly roll fashion. Tuck the ends underneath. Place the roll seam side down in the buttered pan. Repeat to form additional rolls until all the filling is used, placing each roll next to the previous one. Brush the tops with the melted butter. Cut the top layers of the filo diagonally before baking.

Bake at 350° for 40 to 50 minutes, or until the filo is crisp and golden brown. Pour the cool syrup over the hot filo. Cool and cover before storing.

Note: This dessert is better if made a day ahead.

*Rose water is found in Middle Eastern and specialty food stores.

NUTTY FIG ROLLS WITH ORANGE SYRUP

◆

Makes 20 to 25 2-inch servings

Syrup

½   cup sugar
1   cup orange juice concentrate, thawed
2   tablespoons lemon juice
1   cup honey
¼   cup orange liqueur, such as triple sec

Filling

4   cups dried figs, stems removed and finely chopped
2   cups pecans, ground

12   ounces prepared nut filling, for cakes, pastries, and desserts*
½   cup sugar
1   teaspoon cinnamon

1   pound filo leaves, thawed and covered with a damp kitchen towel
1   cup butter, clarified and melted

◆

Butter a 7 × 11-inch pan; set aside. Preheat oven to 350°.

Syrup

In a large, heavy saucepan, combine the sugar, orange juice concentrate, and lemon juice. Stir over low heat until the sugar dissolves. Bring the syrup to a boil, then turn the heat down and simmer for 20 to 25 minutes. Turn the heat off and stir in the honey and orange liqueur. Let cool while making the filling.

Filling

In a large bowl combine the figs, pecans, and nut filling. In a small dish mix the sugar and cinnamon; stir into the fig mixture and mix thoroughly.

Lay 1 sheet of filo on a large plastic cutting board. Brush some of the butter on the filo with a pastry brush. Layer a second and a third sheet of filo on top, brushing each one with butter. Put 1 cup of the filling in a long, narrow row along the short end of the filo. Roll up jelly roll fashion. Tuck the ends underneath. Place the roll seam side down in the buttered pan. Repeat to form additional rolls until all the filling is used, placing each roll next to the previous one. Brush the tops with the remaining melted butter. Cut the top layers of the filo diagonally before baking.

*Nut filling is made with various nuts and has a liqueurlike taste. It can be found in the specialty food section of your supermarket.

Bake at 350° for 40 to 50 minutes, or until the filo is crisp and golden brown. Pour the cool syrup over the hot filo. Cool and cover before storing.

Note: This dessert is better if made a day head.

GERMAN CHOCOLATE NUT PIE

◆

Makes 15 2-inch servings

4 ounces German sweet chocolate	½ pound filo leaves, thawed and
3 eggs	covered with a damp
1 egg yolk	kitchen towel
½ cup butter, melted	½ cup butter, clarified and melted
¼ cup sugar	
½ cup dark brown sugar	***Topping***
1 cup dark corn syrup	2 ounces German sweet chocolate
2 teaspoons vanilla extract	2 tablespoons sour cream
⅛ teaspoon salt	
2 cups walnuts (or other nuts),	
chopped	

◆

Butter a 7 × 11-inch pan; set aside. Preheat oven to 300°.

Melt the chocolate in a double boiler over low heat, stirring until smooth. In a large bowl beat the eggs and egg yolk. Stir in the butter, white sugar, brown sugar, corn syrup, vanilla extract, and salt. Stir in the nuts. Stir in the melted chocolate and mix thoroughly.

Place 1 sheet of filo in the bottom of the buttered pan, folding it to fit. Brush some of the butter on the filo with a pastry brush. Layer a second and a third sheet of filo on top, folding them to fit and brushing each one with butter. Spread the chocolate nut mixture evenly on top of the filo. Top with 2 or 3 sheets of folded, buttered filo. Before baking, sprinkle a few drops of water over the top and around the edges of the filo to prevent it from curling.

Bake at 300° for 40 to 50 minutes, or until the custard is set and filo is crisp and golden brown.

Topping
Melt the chocolate in a double boiler over low heat, stirring until smooth. Stir the sour cream into the melted chocolate. Drizzle the chocolate mixture over the filo. Serve warm or cold. Serve topped with whipped cream or ice cream, if desired.

CINNAMON-APPLE CUSTARD PUFFS

Makes 6 3-inch servings

3	cups apples, peeled and grated	½	pound filo leaves, thawed and covered with a damp kitchen towel
½	cup raisins		
1	cup walnuts, chopped		
½	cup sugar	½	cup butter, clarified and melted
1	teaspoon cinnamon		
½	teaspoon nutmeg		***Glaze***
2	cups cream (or light cream)	2	tablespoons butter
¼	cup cornstarch	¼	cup orange marmalade
⅛	teaspoon salt	1	ounce orange juice, frozen concentrate
¼	cup butter		
½	cup sugar	¼	teaspoon cinnamon
6	egg yolks	½	cup powdered sugar
2	teaspoons vanilla extract		
2	teaspoons orange extract		
2	tablespoons orange liqueur		

Butter a 7 × 11-inch pan; set aside. Preheat oven to 350°.

In a large bowl combine the apples, raisins, and walnuts. In a small dish mix the sugar, cinnamon, and nutmeg. Stir the sugar mixture into the apples. Set aside.

In a double boiler combine the cream, cornstarch, and salt. Stir until the cornstarch dissolves. Stir in the butter and sugar. Cook over—not immersed in—boiling water. Continue stirring until the butter melts. In a mixing bowl, beat egg yolks well; stir in 2 tablespoons of the hot mixture, then mix thoroughly. Stir the yolk mixture into the heated custard. Continue stirring, until smooth and partially thickened. Stir in the vanilla and orange extracts and liqueur. Stir in the apple mixture and thoroughly combine. Remove from the heat and set aside.

Place 1 sheet of filo in the bottom of the buttered pan, folding it to fit. Brush some of the butter on the filo with a pastry brush. Layer 2 or 3 more sheets of folded, buttered filo on top. Spread the custard on the filo. Top with 2 or 3 folded, buttered sheets of filo. Before baking, sprinkle a few drops of water over the top and around the edges of the filo to prevent it from curling.

Bake at 350° for 40 to 50 minutes, or until the custard is set and the filo is golden brown and crisp. Cool on a wire rack while making the glaze.

Glaze

Melt the butter over low heat in a small saucepan. Stir in the orange marmalade, orange juice, cinnamon, and powdered sugar. Stir until hot and bubbly. Drizzle the glaze over the hot filo. Serve warm or cold.

CARAMEL-PEAR STRUDEL

Serves 8

6   medium pears, peeled and sliced
2   tablespoons cornstarch
½   cup brown sugar
1   teaspoon cinnamon
¼   teaspoon nutmeg
¼   teaspoon allspice
1   teaspoon lemon extract
1   teaspoon orange extract
1   teaspoon vanilla extract
1   cup walnuts, chopped
½   cup raisins

½   pound filo leaves, thawed and covered with a damp kitchen towel
½   cup butter, clarified and melted

Glaze

2   teaspoons cornstarch
2   tablespoons frozen orange juice concentrate, thawed
¼   cup orange marmalade
¼   cup walnuts, chopped

Butter a 7 × 11-inch pan; set aside. Preheat oven to 350°.

Put the pears in a large bowl. In a small bowl, mix together the cornstarch, brown sugar, cinnamon, nutmeg, and allspice. Stir the spice mixture into the pears. Stir in the lemon, orange, and vanilla extracts. Stir in the walnuts and raisins, mix thoroughly and set aside.

Place 1 sheet of filo in the bottom of the buttered pan, folding it to fit. Brush some of the butter on the filo with a pastry brush. Layer a second and a third sheet of filo on top. Spread the pear mixture evenly on the filo. Top with 2 or 3 sheets of folded, buttered filo. Before baking, sprinkle a few drops of water over the top and around the edges of the filo to prevent it from curling.

Bake at 350° for 40 to 50 minutes, or until the filo is crisp and golden brown. Cool on a wire rack while making the glaze.

Glaze

In a small saucepan, dissolve the cornstarch in the orange juice. Stir in the marmalade. Stir over low heat, until smooth, hot, bubbly, and thickened. Pour the glaze over the filo and sprinkle the walnuts on top. Serve warm or cold.

CALIFORNIA CHOCOLATE AND ALMOND SQUARES

◆

Makes 16 3-inch servings

24 ounces cream cheese, at room temperature
¾ cup sugar
½ cup amaretto
2 teaspoons almond extract
1 teaspoon vanilla extract
1 teaspoon lemon extract
2 eggs
1 cup almonds, toasted and chopped or sliced, divided
2 cups (about 15) chocolate cookies, crushed
½ pound filo leaves, thawed and covered with a damp kitchen towel

½ cup butter, clarified and melted

Glaze
4 teaspoons cornstarch
2 teaspoons lemon juice
1 ounce frozen orange juice concentrate, thawed
¼ cup orange marmalade
½ teaspoon almond extract

Chocolate Topping
2 tablespoons butter
1 tablespoon milk
1 tablespoon cocoa powder
¾ cup powdered sugar

◆

Butter a 9 × 13-inch pan; set aside. Preheat oven to 350°.

In a large bowl combine the cream cheese, sugar, amaretto, almond extract, vanilla extract, and lemon extract. Beat with an electric mixer until well blended. Add the eggs and almonds, and thoroughly combine. Set aside.

Place 1 sheet of filo in the bottom of the buttered pan, folding it to fit. Brush some of the butter on the filo with a pastry brush. Layer a second and a third sheet of filo on top, folding them to fit and brushing each one with butter. Sprinkle half of the cookie crumbs over the filo. Spread half of the amaretto mixture on. Layer 3 more sheets of folded, buttered filo over the amaretto mixture. Sprinkle the remaining cookie crumbs on top. Spread on the remaining amaretto mixture. Top with 3 or 4 sheets of folded, buttered filo. Before baking, sprinkle a few drops of water over the top and around the edges of the filo to prevent it from curling.

Bake at 350° for 40 to 50 minutes, or until the filo is crisp and golden brown. Cool on a wire rack while making the glaze.

Glaze
In a small saucepan dissolve the cornstarch in the lemon and orange juice. Stir in the marmalade. Cook and stir over low heat until smooth and thickened. Remove from the heat and stir in the almond extract. Sprinkle the almonds over the filo. Drizzle the glaze over the almonds and filo.

Chocolate Topping

Melt the butter over low heat in a small saucepan. Stir in the milk. Combine the cocoa and powdered sugar in a small dish then stir it into the melted butter. Continue stirring until hot and bubbly. Drizzle the chocolate over the top. Serve warm or cold.

PEACH AND WALNUT STRUDEL

◆

Makes 10 to 12 2-inch servings

4 cups peaches, peeled and sliced	1 pound filo leaves, thawed and
1 cup walnuts, finely chopped	covered with a damp
¾ cup sugar	kitchen towel
1 teaspoon cinnamon	1 cup butter, clarified and melted
2 teaspoons lemon peel, finely	**Glaze**
grated	1 tablespoon butter
1 teaspoon vanilla extract	¼ cup peach preserves
1 cup peach preserves	½ cup powdered sugar
1 cup bread crumbs	¼ cup walnuts, chopped

◆

Butter a 7 × 11-inch pan; set aside. Preheat oven to 350°.

In a large bowl combine the peaches, walnuts, and sugar. Stir in the cinnamon, lemon peel, and vanilla extract. Mix thoroughly.

Lay 1 sheet of filo on a large plastic cutting board. Brush some of the butter on the filo with a pastry brush. Layer a second and a third sheet of filo on top, brushing each with butter. Spread a thin layer of the peach preserves on the buttered filo. Sprinkle about ¼ cup of the bread crumbs over the preserves. Put about 1 cup of the peach mixture in a long row at narrow end of the filo. Roll up jelly roll fashion. Tuck the ends underneath. Place the roll seam side down in the buttered pan. Repeat to form additional rolls until all of the filling has been used, placing each roll next to the previous one. Brush the tops and ends with the remaining melted butter.

Bake at 350° for 40 to 50 minutes, or until the filo is crisp and golden brown. Serve hot or cold. Serve with ice cream if desired.

Glaze

Melt the butter over low heat in a small saucepan. Stir in the preserves and powdered sugar. Continue stirring until hot and bubbly. Spread evenly on the warm filo. Sprinkle the walnuts on top.

STRAWBERRIES, CREAM, AND ALMOND CUSTARD PUFFS

Makes 6 3-inch servings

2   cups cream (or light cream)
¼   cup cornstarch
⅛   teaspoon salt
2   tablespoons butter
¾   cup sugar
6   egg yolks
2   teaspoons vanilla extract
1   teaspoon almond extract
2   tablespoons vanilla-flavored
        liqueur (such as Tuaca)
⅓   cup almonds, chopped
½   pound filo leaves, thawed and
        covered with a damp
        kitchen towel

½   cup butter, clarified and melted

Glaze
1   tablespoon cornstarch
½   cup water
½   cup sugar
1   pint strawberries, fresh, washed,
        hulled and sliced
1   teaspoon almond extract
2   tablespoons almonds, chopped

Butter a 7 × 11-inch pan; set aside. Preheat oven to 350°.

In a double boiler, combine the cream, cornstarch, and salt. Stir until the cornstarch dissolves. Stir in the butter and sugar. Cook over—not immersed in—boiling water. Continue stirring until the butter melts. In a mixing bowl, thoroughly beat egg yolks; stir in 2 tablespoons of the hot mixture and mix thoroughly. Stir the yolk mixture into the heated custard. Continue stirring until smooth and partially thickened. Stir in the vanilla extract, almond extract, liqueur, and almonds. Remove from heat and set aside.

Place 1 sheet of filo in the bottom of the buttered pan, folding it to fit. Brush some of the butter on the filo with a pastry brush. Layer a second and a third sheet of filo on top, folding them to fit the pan and brushing each one with butter. Pour the custard on the filo and spread it evenly. Top with 2 or 3 folded, buttered sheets of filo. Before baking, sprinkle a few drops of water over the top and around the edges of the filo to prevent it from curling.

Bake at 350° for 40 to 50 minutes, or until the custard is set and the filo is golden brown and crisp. Cool on a wire rack while making the glaze.

Glaze
In a saucepan, dissolve the cornstarch in the water. Stir in the sugar and a little more than half of the strawberries. Continue stirring over low heat until the

mixture thickens. Remove the cooked berries with a slotted spoon. Stir in the almond extract. When the filo has cooled arrange the rest of the sliced berries on the top and pour the glaze over them. Top with the almonds. Serve warm or cold.

STRAWBERRY DELIGHT

◆

Makes 16 to 18 2-inch servings

1	quart fresh strawberries, washed, hulled, and sliced	1	cup butter, clarified and melted
1	cup sugar	2	cups bread crumbs, divided
2	teaspoons vanilla extract		***Glaze***
1	teaspoon lemon extract	1	tablespoon butter
2	teaspoons lemon peel, grated	⅓	cup strawberry preserves
3	egg yolks, well beaten	1	cup powdered sugar
1	pound filo leaves, thawed and covered with a damp kitchen towel	1	cup strawberries, washed, hulled, and sliced
		½	cup nuts, chopped

◆

Butter a 9 × 13-inch pan; set aside. Preheat oven to 350°.

In a large bowl combine the strawberries, sugar, vanilla extract, lemon extract, and lemon peel; mix thoroughly. Stir in the egg yolks and set aside.

Lay 1 sheet of filo on a large plastic cutting board. Brush some of the butter on the filo with a pastry brush. Layer a second and a third sheet of filo on top, brushing each one with butter. Sprinkle ½ cup of the bread crumbs over the filo. Put 1 cup of the strawberry mixture in a long, narrow row at the short end of the filo. Roll up jelly roll fashion. Tuck the ends underneath. Place the roll seam side down in the buttered pan. Repeat to form additional rolls until all the filling is used, placing each roll next to the previous one. Brush the tops and ends with the remaining melted butter.

Bake at 350° for 40 to 50 minutes, or until the filo is crisp and golden brown. Cool on a wire rack while making the glaze.

Glaze
Melt the butter over low heat in a small saucepan. Stir in the preserves and powdered sugar. Continue stirring until hot and bubbly. Spread evenly on top of the warm filo. Decorate with the strawberries and nuts. Cut the rolls diagonally and serve warm or cold. Serve plain or with ice cream, if desired.

ALMOND CUSTARD BAKLAVA

Makes 10 to 12 2-inch servings

Syrup

1¼ cups sugar
½ cup water
2 tablespoons lemon juice
2 tablespoons amaretto
½ cup honey

Filling

1 cup cream
2 tablespoons cornstarch
⅛ teaspoon salt
½ cup sugar
2 tablespoons butter

3 egg yolks
1 teaspoon almond extract
2 tablespoons amaretto

½ pound filo leaves, thawed and covered with a damp kitchen towel
1 cup butter, clarified and melted
½ pound kataife, thawed* and covered with a damp kitchen towel
2 cups almonds, ground

Butter a 7 × 11-inch pan; set aside. Preheat oven to 350°.

Syrup

In a large heavy saucepan combine the sugar, water, and lemon juice. Stir over low heat until the sugar dissolves. Bring the syrup to a boil, then turn the heat down and simmer for 15 minutes. Stir in the amaretto and honey. Let cool while making the filling.

Filling

In a double boiler, combine the cream, cornstarch, and salt. Stir until the cornstarch dissolves. Cook over—not immersed in—boiling water. Stir in the sugar and butter. Continue stirring until the butter melts. In a mixing bowl, beat the egg yolks well; stir in 2 tablespoons of the hot mixture and mix thoroughly. Stir the yolk mixture into the heated cream. Continue stirring until smooth and partially thickened. Stir the almond extract and amaretto into the mixture. Remove from heat and set aside.

Place 1 sheet of filo in the bottom of the buttered pan, folding it to fit. Brush some of the butter on the filo with a pastry brush. Layer 1 or 2 more sheets of folded, buttered filo in the pan. Tear ½ of the kataife into shreds and place over the filo. Butter the kataife with the melted butter. Spread the custard over the kataife. Sprinkle the nuts over the custard. Tear the remaining kataife into shreds and lay it evenly over the nuts. Butter the top of the kataife. Top with 2 or 3 sheets of folded, buttered filo. Cut the top layers of the filo diagonally before baking. Before baking, sprinkle a few drops of water over the top and around the edges of the filo to prevent it from curling.

*Kataife is found in Middle Eastern or specialty food stores.

Bake at 350° for 40 to 50 minutes, or until the filo is crisp and golden brown. Pour the cool syrup over the hot baklava. When cool, complete the previously begun diagonal cuts, by cutting through the bottom layers of the filo. Rotate the pan one-quarter of a turn and cut the filo in straight rows to form diamond-shaped servings. Cover before storing.

NOTE: This dessert is better if made a day ahead.

BLUEBERRY TART

◆

Makes 6 3-inch servings

½ cup butter, melted
1 cup sugar
6 eggs
2 teaspoons vanilla extract
1 teaspoon lemon extract
2 tablespoons white vinegar
½ cup almonds, chopped
1 cup blueberries (fresh or canned)

½ pound filo leaves, thawed and covered with a damp kitchen towel
½ cup butter, clarified and melted
Glaze
2 tablespoons butter
¾ cup powdered sugar
1 tablespoon amaretto
¼ cup almonds, chopped

◆

Butter a 6 × 10-inch pan; set aside. Preheat oven to 325°.

In a large mixing bowl combine the melted butter, sugar, and eggs, beating with a mixer. Stir in the vanilla extract, lemon extract, and vinegar. Fold in the almonds and blueberries. Set aside.

Place 1 sheet of filo in the bottom of the buttered pan, folding it to fit. Brush some of the butter on the filo with a pastry brush. Layer a second and a third sheet of folded, buttered filo on top. Pour the mixture evenly over the filo. Top with 3 or 4 sheets of folded, buttered filo. Before baking, sprinkle a few drops of water over the top and around the edges of the filo to prevent it from curling.

Bake at 325° for 50 to 60 minutes, or until the filling is set and the filo is golden brown and crisp. Place on a wire rack while making the glaze.

Glaze
Melt the butter over low heat in a small saucepan. Stir in the powdered sugar and amaretto and continue stirring until hot and bubbly. Drizzle the glaze over the warm filo and sprinkle the almonds on top. Serve hot or cold.

WHITE CHOCOLATE AND CRÈME DE MENTHE STRUDEL

◆

Makes 10 2-inch servings

24 ounces cream cheese, at room temperature	½ pound filo leaves, thawed and covered with a damp kitchen towel
1 cup sugar	½ cup butter, clarified and melted
4 egg yolks	
¼ cup cornstarch	***Glaze***
¼ cup crème de menthe (green)	1 tablespoon butter
½ teaspoon mint extract	2 tablespoons crème de menthe
¼ cup white chocolate liqueur	½ cup powdered sugar
1 teaspoon vanilla extract	***Topping***
5 ounces white chocolate	1 tablespoon butter
2 tablespoons sour cream	1 ounce white chocolate

◆

Butter a 7 × 11-inch pan; set aside. Preheat oven to 350°.

In a large bowl combine the cream cheese, sugar, egg yolks, and cornstarch. Beat with an electric mixer until creamy. Put half the cream cheese mixture in a smaller bowl.

Stir the crème de menthe and mint extract into the cream cheese mixture in the smaller bowl, mixing thoroughly. Set aside.

Stir the white chocolate liqueur and vanilla extract into the cream cheese in the large bowl, and mix thoroughly. Break the white chocolate into pieces and melt in a double boiler set over low heat, stirring until smooth and melted. Stir the sour cream into the melted chocolate. Combine the melted chocolate and the white chocolate liqueur mixtures, mixing thoroughly; set aside.

Place 1 sheet of filo in the bottom of the buttered pan, folding it to fit. Brush some of the butter on the filo with a pastry brush. Layer a second and a third sheet of filo on top, folding them to fit and brushing each one with butter. Put the crème de menthe mixture on the filo, spreading it out evenly. Layer two folded, buttered sheets of filo over the mixture. Spread the chocolate mixture on the filo. Top with 2 or 3 sheets of folded, buttered filo. Before baking, sprinkle a few drops of water over the top and around the edges of the filo to prevent it from curling.

Bake at 350° for 40 to 50 minutes or until crisp and golden brown. Cool on a wire rack while making the glaze.

Glaze

Melt the butter over low heat in a small saucepan. Stir in the creme de menthe and powdered sugar. Continue stirring until hot and bubbly. Drizzle the glaze over the filo.

Topping

In another small saucepan, stir while melting the butter and white chocolate over low heat. Continue stirring until the chocolate melts and the mixture is smooth. Drizzle over the filo. Serve cold.

MINI APPLE ROLLS

◆

Makes 6 to 8 2-inch servings

2	large tart apples, peeled, cored, and diced	2	tablespoons flour
¼	cup sugar	2	tablespoons oatmeal
½	teaspoon cinnamon	3	tablespoons butter, melted
¼	teaspoon nutmeg	¼	cup walnuts, chopped
1	tablespoon cornstarch	½	pound filo leaves, thawed and covered with a damp kitchen towel
2	tablespoons butter, melted		
⅓	cup brown sugar	½	cup butter, clarified and melted

◆

Butter a 6 × 10-inch pan; set aside. Preheat oven to 350°.

In a medium bowl, combine the apples, sugar, cinnamon, nutmeg, cornstarch, and butter; mix thoroughly. Set aside.

In a small bowl combine the brown sugar, flour, and oatmeal. Add the melted butter and mix thoroughly. Stir in the nuts.

Lay 1 sheet of filo on a large plastic cutting board. Fold the sheet of filo in half lengthwise to form a rectangle. Brush some of the butter on the filo with a pastry brush. Put about ¾ cup of filling in a long, narrow row along the long end of the filo. Roll up jelly roll fashion. Tuck the ends underneath. Place the roll seam side down in the buttered pan. Repeat to form additional rolls until all the filling is used, placing each roll next to the previous one. Brush the tops and ends with the remaining melted butter. Sprinkle the brown sugar mixture over the rolls before baking.

Bake at 350° for 40 to 50 minutes, or until the filo is crisp and golden brown. Cut the rolls diagonally before serving. Serve warm or cold, with whipped cream or ice cream, if desired.

GREEN APPLE AND DATE STRUDEL

◆

Makes 15 2-inch servings

Syrup
½ cup brown sugar
1 cup apple juice
2 tablespoons lemon juice
1 cup honey

Filling
1 cup walnuts, ground
1 cup dates, finely chopped
3 cups green apples, shredded
3 tablespoons sugar

1 teaspoon cinnamon
¼ teaspoon nutmeg

1 pound filo leaves, thawed and
     covered with a damp
     kitchen towel
1 cup butter, clarified and melted

◆

Butter a 7 × 11-inch pan; set aside. Preheat oven to 350°.

Syrup
In a large, heavy saucepan combine the sugar, apple juice, and lemon juice. Stir over low heat until the sugar dissolves. Bring the syrup to a boil, then decrease heat and simmer for 20 minutes. Stir in the honey. Let cool while making the filling.

Filling
In a large bowl combine the walnuts, dates, and apples. In a cup, mix the sugar, cinnamon, and nutmeg; pour over the nut and apple mixture and mix thoroughly.

Lay 1 sheet of filo on a large plastic cutting board. Brush some of the butter on the filo with a pastry brush. Layer a second and a third sheet of filo on top, brushing each with butter. Put 1 cup of mixture in a long row at narrow end of the filo. Roll up jelly roll fashion. Tuck the ends underneath. Place the roll seam side down in the buttered pan. Repeat to form additional rolls until all the filling has been used, placing each roll next to the previous one. Brush the tops with the remaining melted butter. Cut the top layers of filo diagonally before baking.

Bake at 350° for 40 to 50 minutes, or until the filo is crisp and golden brown. Pour the cool syrup over the hot filo. Cool and cover before storing.

Note: This dessert is better if made a day ahead.

AMARETTO CUSTARD PUFFS

◆

Makes 6 3-inch servings

2	cups cream (or light cream)	½	pound filo leaves, thawed and covered with a damp kitchen towel
¼	cup cornstarch		
⅛	teaspoon salt		
¼	cup butter	½	cup butter, clarified and melted
¾	cup sugar		
6	egg yolks		***Glaze***
2	teaspoons almond extract	1	tablespoon butter
2	tablespoons amaretto	½	cup powdered sugar
½	cup almonds, toasted and chopped	2	tablespoons amaretto
		¼	cup almonds

◆

Butter a 6 × 10-inch pan; set aside. Preheat oven to 350°.

In a double boiler, stir together the cream, cornstarch, and salt. Stir until the cornstarch dissolves. Cook over—not immersed in—boiling water. Stir in the butter and sugar. Continue stirring until the butter melts. In a mixing bowl, beat egg yolks thoroughly; stir in two tablespoons of the hot mixture and mix well. Stir the yolk mixture into the heated cream mixture. Continue stirring until smooth and partially thickened. Stir the almond extract, amaretto, and almonds into the mixture. Remove from heat and set aside.

Place 1 sheet of filo in the bottom of the buttered pan, folding it to fit. Brush some of the butter on the filo with a pastry brush. Layer 2 or 3 more sheets of folded, buttered filo. Pour the custard evenly over the filo. Top with 2 or 3 folded, buttered sheets of filo. Before baking, sprinkle a few drops of water over the top and around the edges of the filo to prevent it from curling.

Bake at 350° for 40 to 50 minutes, or until the custard is set and the filo is golden brown and crisp. Cool on a wire rack while making the glaze.

Glaze

Melt the butter in a saucepan over low heat. Stir in the powdered sugar and amaretto, mixing thoroughly. Continue stirring until hot and bubbly. Drizzle the glaze on the warm filo. Sprinkle the almonds over the top. Serve warm or cold.

CHOCOLATE TOFFEE SQUARES

Makes 12 2-inch servings

1 cup semisweet chocolate chips
24 ounces cream cheese, at room
    temperature, divided
½ cup sugar
1 teaspoon vanilla extract
2 egg yolks
¼ cup sour cream
¼ cup coffee-flavored liqueur
2 teaspoons instant coffee,
    dissolved in 1 tablespoon
    hot water
½ cup dark brown sugar
2 tablespoons dark corn syrup
1 tablespoon cornstarch
1 pound filo leaves, thawed and
    covered with a damp
    kitchen towel

1 cup butter, clarified and melted

Glaze

½ cup powdered sugar
1 teaspoons instant coffee,
    dissolved in 1 teaspoon hot
    water
1 tablespoon coffee-flavored liqueur

Additional Topping

⅓ cup semisweet chocolate chips
1 tablespoon sour cream
1 tablespoon powdered sugar

Butter a 7 × 11-inch pan; set aside. Preheat oven to 350°.

Melt the chocolate chips in a double boiler over low heat, stirring until smooth. In a medium bowl combine 12 ounces of the cream cheese, sugar, vanilla extract, and 1 egg yolk. Beat with an electric mixer until thoroughly blended. Add the sour cream and melted chocolate chips and beat well with the mixer until thoroughly blended. Set aside.

In another medium bowl, combine the rest of the cream cheese, coffee liqueur, dissolved instant coffee, brown sugar, corn syrup, cornstarch, and the other egg yolk. Mix thoroughly with the mixer. Set aside.

Place 1 sheet of filo in the bottom of the buttered pan, folding it to fit. Brush some of the butter on the filo with a pastry brush. Layer a second and a third sheet of folded, buttered filo on top. Spread the chocolate-cream cheese mixture evenly over the filo. Layer 2 more folded, buttered sheets of filo on top of the filling. Spread the coffee mixture over the filo. Top with 2 or 3 sheets of folded, buttered filo. Before baking, sprinkle a few drops of water over the top and around the edges of the filo to prevent it from curling.

Bake at 350° for 40 to 50 minutes, or until the filo is crisp and golden brown. Cool thoroughly on a wire rack while making the glaze.

Glaze

Combine the powdered sugar, dissolved coffee, and liqueur in a small saucepan. Stir over low heat, until smooth, hot and bubbly. Drizzle the glaze over the cooled filo.

Topping

Melt the chocolate chips in a double boiler over low heat, stirring until smooth. Add the sour cream and powdered sugar to the melted chocolate chips and mix thoroughly. Drizzle the melted chocolate over the filo, creating a design. Chill. Serve cold.

PECAN ROLLS

◆

Makes 16 to 18 2-inch servings

Syrup		Filling	
¾	cup butter	4	cups pecans, ground
1	cup sugar	3	eggs, well beaten
1	cup dark brown sugar	1	pound filo leaves, thawed and covered with a damp kitchen towel
2	cups dark corn syrup		
½	teaspoon salt	1	cup butter, clarified and melted

◆

Butter a 9 × 13-inch pan; set aside. Preheat oven to 300°.

Syrup

Melt the butter over low heat in a large, heavy saucepan. Stir in the white sugar, brown sugar, corn syrup, and salt. Continue stirring until the sugar dissolves. Set aside.

Filling

In a large bowl combine the pecans, reserving ½ cup for the top of the rolls. Stir in half of the syrup mixture. Mix thoroughly. Stir in the eggs and mix thoroughly.

Lay 1 sheet of filo on a large plastic cutting board. Brush some of the butter on the filo with a pastry brush. Layer a second and a third sheet of filo on top, brushing each with butter. Put 1 cup of the filling in a long, narrow row at the short end of the filo. Roll up jelly roll fashion. Tuck the ends underneath. Place the roll seam side down in the buttered pan. Repeat to form additional rolls until all the filling is used, placing each roll next to the previous one. Brush the tops and ends with the remaining melted butter. Sprinkle the reserved pecans on top of the rolls. Cut the top layers of filo diagonally before baking.

Bake at 300° for 50 to 60 minutes, or until the filo is crisp and golden brown. Pour the cooled syrup over the hot pecan rolls. Serve warm or cold with whipped cream or ice cream, if desired. Cool and cover before storing.

BLACK AND WHITE COOLER

Makes 10 3-inch servings

24 ounces cream cheese, divided, at room temperature	1 pound filo leaves, thawed and covered with a damp kitchen towel
¼ cup sour cream	
¾ cup sugar, divided	1 cup butter, clarified and melted
1½ teaspoons vanilla extract	
2 egg yolks, divided	***Glaze***
⅓ cup sour cream	1 tablespoon sour cream
1 cup semisweet chocolate chips	⅓ cup milk chocolate chips, melted

◆

Butter a 7 × 11-inch pan; set aside. Preheat oven to 350°.

Put 12 ounces cream cheese, ¼ cup sour cream, ¼ cup sugar, vanilla extract, and 1 egg yolk in a medium bowl. Beat with an electric mixer until creamy and set aside.

Put the rest of the cream cheese, ⅓ cup sour cream, ½ cup sugar, and 1 egg yolk in a slightly larger bowl. Beat until creamy. Melt the chocolate chips in a double boiler over low heat, stirring continuously. Add the melted chocolate to the cream cheese mixture and set aside.

Place 1 sheet of filo in the bottom of the buttered pan, folding it to fit. Brush some of the butter on the filo with a pastry brush. Layer a second and a third sheet of folded, buttered filo on top. Put the chocolate mixture on the filo, spreading it out evenly. Layer 2 folded, buttered sheets of filo over the chocolate mixture. Put the vanilla mixture on, spreading it out evenly. Top with 2 or 3 sheets of folded, buttered filo. Brush the top with the remaining melted butter. Before baking, sprinkle a few drops of water over the top and around the edges of the filo to prevent it from curling.

Bake at 350° for 40 to 50 minutes, or until the filo is crisp and golden brown. Cool thoroughly on a wire rack while making the glaze.

Glaze
Melt the chocolate chips in a double boiler over low heat, stirring continuously. Stir the sour cream into the melted chocolate. Drizzle the chocolate mixture over the filo creating a design. Chill. Serve cold.

❖❖❖

NECTARINE-RAISIN SQUARES

◆

Makes 8 to 10 2-inch servings

4	cups nectarines, peeled and sliced	1	pound filo leaves, thawed and covered with a damp kitchen towel
½	cup raisins		
½	cup walnuts, chopped	1	cup butter, clarified and melted powdered sugar (optional)
¾	cup sugar		
2	tablespoons cornstarch		
2	cups bread crumbs		***Peach Glaze***
½	cup peach schnapps	1	tablespoon butter
1	teaspoon cinnamon	¼	cup peach preserves
2	teaspoons vanilla extract	¼	cup powdered sugar
2	teaspoons orange extract	2	tablespoons walnuts, chopped
1	teaspoon lemon extract		

◆

Butter a 7 × 11-inch pan; set aside. Preheat oven to 350°.

In a large bowl combine the nectarines, raisins, walnuts, sugar, and cornstarch; mix thoroughly. Stir in the bread crumbs, peach schnapps, cinnamon, vanilla extract, orange extract, and lemon extract. Mix thoroughly.

Place 1 sheet of filo in the bottom of the buttered pan, folding it to fit. Brush some of the butter on the filo with a pastry brush. Layer a second and a third sheet of filo on top, folding them to fit and brushing each one with butter. Put the nectarine mixture on the filo, spreading it evenly. Top with 2 or 3 sheets of folded, buttered filo. Before baking, sprinkle a few drops of water over the top and around the edges of the filo to prevent it from curling.

Bake at 350° for 40 to 50 minutes, or until the filo is crisp and golden brown. Cool on a wire rack. Dust with powdered sugar, if desired, or serve with the glaze.

Glaze

Melt the butter over low heat in a small saucepan. Stir in the peach preserves and powdered sugar. Continue stirring until hot and bubbly. Spread the hot glaze on the warm filo. Sprinkle the walnuts on evenly. Serve warm or cold. Serve with whipped cream or ice cream, if desired.

ORANGE AND PRUNE CUSTARD PUFFS

Makes 8 3-inch servings

24	ounces prunes, pits removed and finely chopped	2	teaspoons orange extract
⅓	cup orange liqueur	1	cup walnuts, chopped
2	cups cream or light cream	½	pound filo leaves, thawed and covered with a damp kitchen towel
1	cup frozen orange juice concentrate, thawed	½	cup butter, clarified and melted
¼	cup cornstarch		
⅛	teaspoon salt		**Glaze**
¼	cup butter	1	tablespoon butter
14	ounces sweetened condensed milk	½	cup powdered sugar
6	egg yolks	¼	cup orange marmalade

Butter a 7 × 11-inch pan; set aside. Preheat oven to 350°.

Put the prunes in a medium bowl and pour the orange liqueur over them. Let this soak while preparing the custard. In a double boiler, combine the cream, orange juice, cornstarch, and salt. Stir until the cornstarch dissolves. Stir in the butter and condensed milk. Cook over—not immersed in—boiling water. Continue stirring until the butter melts. In a mixing bowl, beat egg yolks thoroughly; stir in two tablespoons of the hot mixture and mix well. Stir the yolk mixture into the heated custard. Continue stirring until smooth and partially thickened. Stir in the orange extract, prunes and liqueur, and walnuts. Remove from heat and set aside.

Place 1 sheet of filo in the bottom of the buttered pan, folding it to fit. Brush some of the butter on the filo with a pastry brush. Layer a second and a third sheet of filo on top, folding them to fit and brushing each one with butter. Pour the custard evenly over the filo. Top with 2 or 3 folded, buttered sheets of filo. Before baking, sprinkle a few drops of water over the top and around the edges of the filo to prevent it from curling.

Bake at 350° for 40 to 50 minutes, or until the custard is set and the filo is golden brown and crisp. Cool on a wire rack while making the glaze.

Glaze

Melt the butter over low heat in a small saucepan. Stir in the powdered sugar and marmalade. Continue stirring until smooth, hot, and bubbly. Drizzle the glaze over the filo. Serve warm or cold.

❖◆❖

APRICOT HONEY STRUDEL

◆

Makes 20 to 25 2-inch servings

Syrup

1	cup sugar
1	cup apricot nectar
2	tablespoons lemon juice
2	teaspoons orange extract
1	cup honey
2	tablespoons orange liqueur

Filling

2	cups dried apricots, chopped fine
1	cup dates, chopped fine

1	cup walnuts, ground
1	cup almonds, ground
1	cup coconut, grated
3	tablespoons sugar
1	teaspoon cinnamon

1	pound filo leaves, thawed and covered with a damp kitchen towel
1	cup butter, clarified and melted

◆

Butter a 7 × 11-inch pan; set aside. Preheat oven to 350°.

Syrup

In a large heavy saucepan combine the sugar, apricot nectar, and lemon juice. Stir over low heat, until the sugar dissolves. Bring the syrup to a boil, then turn the heat down and simmer for 20 to 25 minutes. Stir in the orange extract, honey, and orange liqueur. Let cool while making the filling.

Filling

In a large bowl put the apricots, dates, walnuts, almonds, and coconut. In a cup mix the sugar and cinnamon. Pour this mixture over the apricot mixture and mix thoroughly.

Place 1 sheet of filo in the bottom of the buttered pan, folding it to fit. Brush some of the butter on the filo with a pastry brush. Layer a second and a third sheet of filo on top, folding them to fit and brushing each one with butter. Put about 1 cup of the filling in a long narrow row at the short end of the filo. Roll up jelly roll fashion. Tuck the ends underneath. Place the roll seam side down in the buttered pan. Repeat to form additional rolls until all the filling is used, placing each roll next to the previous one. Brush the tops with the melted butter. Cut the top layers of filo diagonally before baking.

Bake at 350° for 40 to 50 minutes, or until the filo is crisp and golden brown. Pour the cool syrup over the hot filo. When cooled, finish cutting through the bottom layers of the previously cut filo. Rotate the pan one-quarter of a turn, and cut the filo in straight rows to make diamond-shaped servings. Cool thoroughly and cover before storing.

Note: This dessert is best when made a day ahead.

AUTUMN PUMPKIN STRUDEL

Makes 12 3-inch servings

12 ounces cream cheese, at room temperature
⅓ cup sugar
4 teaspoons vanilla extract, divided
3 egg yolks, divided
16 ounces pumpkin, canned, divided
½ cup brown sugar
¼ cup white sugar
2 tablespoons cocoa powder
⅓ cup brown sugar
½ teaspoon cinnamon
¼ teaspoon nutmeg

¼ teaspoon ginger
1 pound filo leaves, thawed and covered with a damp kitchen towel
1 cup butter, clarified and melted

Glaze
1 tablespoon butter, melted
1 teaspoon vanilla extract
1 tablespoon milk
½ cup powdered sugar
¼ cup pecans, chopped

Butter a 7 × 11-inch pan; set aside. Preheat oven to 300°.

In a medium bowl combine the cream cheese, ⅓ cup sugar, 2 teaspoons vanilla extract, and 1 egg yolk. Beat with an electric mixer until thoroughly mixed. Set aside.

In another medium bowl combine 8 ounces pumpkin, ½ cup brown sugar, ¼ cup white sugar, cocoa, 1 teaspoon vanilla extract, and 1 egg yolk. Beat thoroughly. Set aside.

In a third medium bowl combine the remaining pumpkin, ⅓ cup brown sugar, cinnamon, nutmeg, ginger, 1 teaspoon vanilla extract, and 1 egg yolk; beat thoroughly. Set aside.

Place 1 sheet of filo in the bottom of the buttered pan, folding it to fit. Brush some of the butter on the filo with a pastry brush. Layer a second and a third sheet of filo on top, folding them to fit and brushing each one with butter. Spoon the cream cheese mixture onto the filo, spreading it out evenly. Layer 2 sheets of folded, buttered filo over the cream cheese mixture. Spread the chocolate-pumpkin mixture on top of the filo. Top with 2 folded, buttered sheets of filo. Spoon the plain pumpkin onto the filo, spreading it evenly. Cover with 2 or 3 sheets of folded, buttered filo. Brush the top with the remaining melted butter. Before baking, sprinkle a few drops of water over the top and around the edges of the filo to prevent it from curling.

Bake at 300° for 50 to 60 minutes, or until the custard is set and the filo is crisp and golden brown. Cool on a wire rack while making the glaze.

Glaze

Melt the butter over low heat in a small saucepan. Stir in the vanilla extract, milk, and powdered sugar. Continue stirring until hot and bubbly. Drizzle the glaze over the filo. Serve warm or cold.

BLACKBERRY-ALMOND STRUDEL

◆

Makes 8 3-inch servings

1 pint blackberries, (fresh or frozen)	½ pound filo leaves, thawed and covered with a damp kitchen towel
⅓ cup almonds, toasted and chopped or slivered	½ cup butter, clarified and melted
¾ cup sugar	
2 tablespoons cornstarch	***Glaze***
½ teaspoon cinnamon	2 tablespoons butter
1 teaspoon almond extract	¾ cup blackberry jam
1 teaspoon lemon extract	¼ cup almonds, toasted and chopped or slivered
2 cups bread crumbs	

◆

Butter a 7 × 11-inch pan; set aside. Preheat oven to 350°.

In a medium bowl combine the blackberries, almonds, sugar, cornstarch, and cinnamon. Stir in the almond extract and lemon extract. Stir in the bread crumbs. Set aside.

Place 1 sheet of filo in the bottom of the buttered pan, folding it to fit. Brush some of the butter on the filo with a pastry brush. Layer a second and a third sheet of folded, buttered filo on top. Spread the blackberry mixture evenly over the filo. Top with 3 or 4 sheets of folded, buttered filo. Before baking, sprinkle a few drops of water over the top and around the edges of the filo to prevent it from curling.

Bake at 350° for 40 to 50 minutes, or until the filo is crisp and golden brown. Cool on a wire rack while making the glaze.

Glaze

Melt the butter over low heat in a small saucepan. Stir in the blackberry jam and continue stirring until hot and bubbly. Remove from the heat. Sprinkle the almonds over the filo. Spread the glaze evenly over the warm filo. Serve warm or cold.

BAKLAVA TORTE

◆

Makes 20 to 25 2-inch servings

Syrup

1 cup sugar
¾ cup water
2 tablespoons lemon juice
1 cup honey
1 tablespoon amaretto

Crust

8 ounces cream cheese, at room
 temperature
¼ cup butter
⅓ cup sugar
1 egg
½ cup flour

1 teaspoon vanilla extract
2 teaspoons almond extract

Filling

2 cups almonds, ground
½ cup coconut, grated
4 egg yolks
½ cup sugar
1 teaspoon cinnamon
4 egg whites

½ pound filo leaves, thawed and
 covered with a damp kitchen towel
½ cup butter, clarified and melted

◆

Butter a 7 × 11-inch pan; set aside. Preheat oven to 350°.

Syrup

In a heavy saucepan combine the sugar, water, and lemon juice. Stir over low heat until the sugar dissolves. Bring the syrup to a boil, then turn the heat down and simmer for 15 to 20 minutes. Stir in the honey and amaretto. Let cool while making the filling.

Crust

In a medium bowl beat the cream cheese, butter, and sugar. In a separate bowl, beat the egg well; add to cream cheese mixture. Add the flour, vanilla extract, almond extract and beat well. Press this mixture into the bottom of the buttered pan to make the crust.

Filling

In a medium bowl combine the almonds and coconut. In another bowl, thoroughly beat the egg yolks. Add to the almond-coconut mixture and mix thoroughly. Set aside. In a cup combine the sugar and cinnamon. In a medium bowl, beat the egg whites with an electric mixer until stiff. Slowly add the sugar and cinnamon mixture. Gently fold the almond-coconut mixture into the egg whites; mixing carefully but thoroughly. Set aside.

Place 1 sheet of filo over the crust in the bottom of the buttered pan, folding it to fit. Brush some of the butter on the filo with a pastry brush. Layer 2 more sheets of buttered, folded filo over the crust. Spoon filling onto the buttered filo, spreading it evenly. Top with 2 or 3 sheets of folded, buttered filo. Cut the top layers of the filo diagonally before baking. Before baking, sprinkle a few drops of water over the top and around the edges of the filo to prevent it from curling.

Bake at 350° for 40 to 50 minutes, or until the filo is crisp and golden brown. Pour the cool syrup over the hot baklava. When cool, complete the previously begun diagonal cuts by cutting through the torte's bottom layers and crust. Rotate the pan one-quarter of a turn and cut the filo in straight rows to make diamond-shaped servings.

Note: This dessert freezes well and is better if made a day ahead.

APPLE STRUDEL

Makes 24 2-inch servings

6 cups Granny Smith apples (about 6 medium), chopped	1 tablespoon vanilla extract
¾ cup brown sugar, packed	1 pound filo leaves, thawed and covered with a damp kitchen towel
¾ cup walnuts, almonds, or pecans, chopped	1½ cups bread cubes, buttered and toasted
½ cup raisins	
1 teaspoon cinnamon	1 cup butter, clarified and melted
2 teaspoons lemon zest, grated	powdered sugar for dusting

◆

Butter a 9 × 13-inch pan; set aside. Preheat oven to 350°.

In a large bowl, combine the chopped apples, brown sugar, nuts, raisins, cinnamon, lemon zest, and vanilla extract; mix thoroughly.

Lay 1 sheet of filo on a large plastic cutting board. Brush some of the butter on the filo with a pastry brush. Layer a second and a third sheet of filo on top, brushing each one with butter. Sprinkle about ½ cup of the bread cubes over the buttered filo. Put about 1 cup of mixture in a long, narrow row at the short end of the filo. Roll up jelly roll fashion. Tuck the ends underneath. Place the roll seam side down in the buttered pan. Repeat to form additional rolls until all the filling is used, placing each roll next to the previous one. Brush the tops and ends with the remaining melted butter.

Bake at 350° for 40 to 50 minutes, or until the filo is crisp and golden brown. Cool on a wire rack and dust with powdered sugar. Cut the rolls diagonally before serving. Serve warm or cold. Serve with whipped cream or ice cream, if desired.

ELEGANT EIGHT-CHOCOLATE
EXTRAORDINAIRE

◆

Makes 24 2-inch servings

Crust

8 ounces cream cheese, at room temperature	1 egg
¼ cup butter	½ cup flour
⅓ cup sugar	2 tablespoons cocoa powder
	1 teaspoon vanilla extract

◆

Butter a 9 × 13-inch pan; set aside. Preheat oven to 300°.

In a medium bowl, with an electric mixer, beat the cream cheese, butter, and sugar. Stir in the egg and beat thoroughly. Add the flour, cocoa, and vanilla extract and beat well. Press this mixture into the bottom of the buttered pan. Set aside.

First Layer

8 ounces cream cheese, at room temperature	1 egg yolk
2 tablespoons sour cream	4 ounces semisweet chocolate chips
⅓ cup sugar	1 ounce crème de cacao
	1 teaspoon vanilla extract

Beat the cream cheese, sour cream, and sugar in a medium bowl with an electric mixer. Stir in the egg yolk and beat thoroughly. Melt the chocolate chips in a double boiler over low heat, stirring until smooth. Add the melted semisweet chocolate chips, creme de cacao, and vanilla extract to the cream cheese mixture. Beat until thoroughly blended and set aside.

Second Layer

8 ounces cream cheese, at room temperature	4 ounces milk chocolate chips
2 tablespoons sour cream	1 ounce Truffles Liqueur de Chocolat (or crème de cacao)
¼ cup sugar	1 teaspoon vanilla extract
1 egg yolk	

Beat the cream cheese, sour cream, and sugar in a medium bowl with an electric mixer. Stir in the egg yolk and beat thoroughly. Melt the chocolate chips in a double boiler over low heat, stirring until smooth. Add the melted milk chocolate, Truffles Liqueur de Chocolat, and vanilla extract to the cream cheese mixture. Beat until thoroughly blended and set aside.

Third Layer

8	ounces cream cheese, at room temperature	1	egg yolk
		4	ounces white chocolate
2	tablespoons sour cream	1	ounce white chocolate liqueur
¼	cup sugar	1	teaspoon vanilla extract

Beat the cream cheese, sour cream, and sugar in a third medium bowl with an electric mixer. Stir in the egg yolk and beat thoroughly. Melt the chocolate in a double boiler over low heat, stirring until smooth. Add the melted white chocolate, white chocolate liqueur, and vanilla extract to the cream cheese mixture. Beat until thoroughly blended and set aside.

½　pound filo leaves, thawed and covered with a damp kitchen towel
½　cup butter, clarified and melted

Place 1 sheet of filo over the crust in the pan, folding it to fit. Brush some of the butter on the filo with a pastry brush. Add a second sheet, folding it and brushing it with butter. Spread the semisweet chocolate mixture, the first layer, evenly on the filo. Layer 1 sheet of folded, buttered filo over the semisweet chocolate mixture. Spread the milk chocolate mixture, the second layer, evenly on the filo. Layer 1 sheet of folded, buttered filo over the milk chocolate mixture. Spread the white chocolate mixture, the third layer, on the filo. Top with 2 sheets of folded, buttered filo. Before baking, sprinkle a few drops of water over the top and around the edges of the filo to prevent it from curling.

Bake at 300° for 50 to 60 minutes, or until the filling is set and the filo is crisp and golden brown. Cool thoroughly on a wire rack while making the topping.

Topping

8	ounces cream cheese, at room temperature	1	tablespoon cocoa powder
		2	ounces German sweet chocolate, grated
1	teaspoon vanilla extract		
¾	cup powdered sugar	⅓	cup pecans, chopped

Put the cream cheese and vanilla extract in a mixing bowl and beat with an electric mixer until creamy. In a small bowl combine the powdered sugar, cocoa powder, and grated German chocolate. Mix until thoroughly blended. Stir the chocolate into the cream cheese and continue beating until blended. Spread over the filo and sprinkle the pecans on top. Serve cold.

PAPAYA-LEMON CREAM PUFFS

Makes 6 3-inch servings

1 cup cream (or light cream)
½ cup lemonade concentrate, thawed
¼ cup cornstarch
⅛ teaspoon salt
¼ cup butter
¾ cup sugar
6 egg yolks
2 teaspoons vanilla extract
1 teaspoon lemon extract
2 cups papaya, purèed

½ pound filo leaves, thawed and covered with a damp kitchen towel
½ cup butter, clarified and melted

Glaze

1 tablespoon butter
2 tablespoons lemonade concentrate, thawed
½ cup powdered sugar

Butter a 7 × 11-inch pan; set aside. Preheat oven to 350°.

In a double boiler, combine the cream, lemonade, cornstarch, and salt. Stir until the cornstarch dissolves. Stir in the butter and sugar. Cook over—not immersed in—boiling water. Continue stirring until the butter melts. In a mixing bowl, beat egg yolks thoroughly; stir in two tablespoons of the hot mixture, then mix thoroughly. Stir the yolk mixture into the heated custard. Continue stirring, until smooth and partially thickened. Stir in the vanilla extract, lemon extract, and papaya and mix thoroughly. Remove from heat and set aside.

Place 1 sheet of filo in the bottom of the buttered pan, folding it to fit. Brush some of the butter on the filo with a pastry brush. Layer a second and a third sheet of filo on top, folding them to fit the pan and brushing each one with butter. Pour the custard on the filo and spread it evenly. Top with 2 or 3 folded, buttered sheets of filo. Before baking, sprinkle a few drops of water over the top and around the edges of the filo to prevent it from curling.

Bake at 350° for 40 to 50 minutes, or until the custard is set and the filo is golden brown and crisp. Cool on a wire rack while making the glaze.

Glaze

Melt the butter over low heat in a small saucepan. Stir in the lemonade and powdered sugar. Continue stirring until smooth, hot, and bubbly. Spread the glaze over the filo. Serve warm or cold.

THE LIGHTER
SIDE
OF FILO

This chapter is geared toward healthier eating. With so many of us cutting back on calories and wanting to eat heart-healthy foods, these recipes address those concerns. They give you alternatives by decreasing the fat and cholesterol contents and by cutting the portions in half.

The food in this section, as in the rest of the book, makes for beautiful presentation. But, the calories in these recipes have been trimmed by using ingredients that contain less fat. You will find that fresh fruit, seafood, and fresh vegetables are key ingredients in these recipes. If you favor a different flavor or ingredient, do not hesitate to substitute it for an ingredient in a recipe.

All of the recipes in *Filo Fantastic* were originally created using clarified butter. This is because it is the butter fat that makes filo flaky, tender, delicate, and so wonderfully rich tasting. But you can use margarine instead of butter with all the recipes in this book; simply clarify the margarine as you would clarify butter and brush it on the filo in the same way. Filo dishes made with margarine lose only a little of the delicate flavor they have when made with butter. There are also several diet margarines on the market that work well with filo. Whether you choose regular or diet margarine, you can enjoy the rich taste of filo without all the cholesterol and fat.

Another way to lower the fat content in appetizers, entrées, and desserts made with filo, is to brush the sheets with canola oil. Canola oil is one of the cooking oils recommended by many respected health-oriented organizations. There is a difference in taste when canola oil is used in place of butter, but the difference is not significant enough to keep cooks from using it. The change in taste is only noticeable when eating a plain, unfilled baked filo shell.

Whether filo is brushed with butter, margarine, or canola oil, it browns the same and attains the same degree of flakiness. And if you're comparing calories, there isn't much difference between butter, margarine, and canola oil. But the difference in the saturated fat per tablespoon is significant because cooking oils are considerably lower in saturated fat than butter or margarine. Another reason for using canola oil, or any other oil recommended by a health professional, is that it eliminates one preparation step (clarifying) and is less expensive than butter or margarine.

To give you the best taste possible and the flakiest pastry, the recipes in this book call for butter. However, as this chapter demonstrates, you can lower the fat and cholesterol contents in any filo dish simply by substituting margarine (regular or diet) or canola oil for butter.

FIERY CHEESE BITES IN FILO CUPS

Makes 25 bite-size servings

25 3-inch squares of foil
6 ounces mozzarella cheese, part skim, grated
12 ounces Mexican-style pasteurized process cheese spread, grated
1 cup light sour cream
¼ cup pimientos, chopped
2 jalapeño peppers, minced

¾ cup onion, chopped
    salt and pepper to taste
½ pound filo leaves, thawed and covered with a damp kitchen towel
¼ cup margarine, clarified and melted (or ¼ cup canola oil with ¼ teaspoon butter flavoring)

Preheat oven to 350°. Line 25 miniature muffin cups with foil squares.

In a large mixing bowl, combine the mozzarella cheese, process cheese, sour cream, pimientos, jalapeño peppers, and onion. Beat with an electric mixer until thoroughly mixed. Add salt and pepper to taste. Refrigerate while making the shells.

Lay 3 sheets of filo on a large plastic cutting board. Using sharp scissors or a sharp knife cut each pastry sheet into 6 3-inch squares. Brush margarine (or canola oil) on 3 of the squares with a pastry brush. Place the squares on top of each other. Gently mold the 3 pastry squares into a muffin cup, leaving a 1-inch overhang. Repeat the process to make the desired number of pastry shells.

Bake at 350° for 10 minutes, or until the shells are crisp and golden brown. Place the muffin pan on a wire rack to cool for 10 minutes before filling the shells.

Carefully put 2 teaspoons of the cheese filling in each shell. Remove the foil before serving. Serve immediately after filling.

MUSHROOM AND SHRIMP IN FILO BOATS

Makes 5 standard- or 15 bite-size servings

5 paper or foil muffin liners (or 15 3-inch squares of foil, for bite-size servings)	½ pound filo leaves, thawed and covered with a damp kitchen towel
1 cup small curd cottage cheese	¼ cup margarine, clarified and melted (or ¼ cup canola oil with ¼ teaspoon butter flavoring)
¼ cup light sour cream	
⅓ cup green onions, finely chopped	
⅓ cup parsley, chopped	½ pound shrimp, cooked and peeled
¼ cup mushrooms, finely chopped	½ cup Parmesan cheese, freshly grated
1 tablespoon black olives, chopped	

◆

Preheat oven to 350°. Put liners in 5 standard-size muffin cups, or for bite-size servings, line 15 miniature muffin cups with foil squares.

In a medium mixing bowl combine the cottage cheese, sour cream, green onions, parsley, mushrooms, and black olives. Thoroughly mix. Refrigerate.

For standard-size servings: Lay 3 sheets of filo on a large plastic cutting board. Using sharp scissors, or a sharp knife, cut each sheet into 4 5-inch squares. Brush margarine (or canola oil) on 3 of the squares with a pastry brush. Place the squares on top of each other. Gently mold the 3 pastry squares into a muffin cup leaving a 1-inch overhang. Repeat the process to make 4 more pastry shells.

For bite-size servings: Follow the above instructions with one exception: cut each of the 3 filo sheets into 6 3-inch squares.

Bake at 350° for 10 minutes, or until the shells are crisp and golden brown. Place the muffin pan on a wire rack to cool for 10 minutes before filling the shells.

For standard-size servings: Carefully put 3 tablespoons of the cottage cheese mixture in each shell. Sprinkle 1 tablespoon of the Parmesan cheese over the filling. Garnish with several shrimp. Remove the liners before serving. Serve immediately after filling.

For bite-size appetizers use ⅓ of the filling used in the standard size. (For example, use 1 tablespoon instead of 3 tablespoons of filling for each shell.)

Note: This makes a wonderful appetizer or light luncheon dish.

SHRIMP AND CRAB IN FILO SHELLS

Serves 10 to 12

12 paper or foil muffin liners
2 cups creamed cottage cheese
½ cup Parmesan cheese, freshly grated
1½ cups tomatoes, finely chopped
2 teaspoons dill weed
½ medium onion, minced
½ pound filo leaves, thawed and covered with a damp kitchen towel

¼ cup margarine, clarified and melted (or ¼ cup canola oil plus ¼ teaspoon butter flavoring)
½ pound shrimp, cooked, peeled, and chilled
6 ounces crab meat, cooked, picked over, and chilled

Preheat oven to 350°. Put liners in 12 standard-size muffin cups.

In a medium bowl combine the cottage cheese and Parmesan cheese. In another medium bowl, combine the tomatoes and dill weed. Stir in the onion and mix thoroughly. Refrigerate ingredients in both bowls until thoroughly chilled.

Lay 3 sheets of filo on a large plastic cutting board. Using sharp scissors, or a sharp knife, cut each pastry sheet into 4 5-inch squares. Brush margarine (or canola oil) on 3 squares of filo with a pastry brush. Place them on top of each other. Gently mold the pastry squares into a muffin cup, leaving a 1-inch overhang. Repeat the process to make the desired number of pastry shells.

Bake at 350° for 10 minutes, or until the shells are crisp and golden brown. Place the muffin pan on a wire rack to cool for 10 minutes before filling the shells.

Carefully put 2 tablespoons of the cottage cheese filling in each shell. Top each dollop of filling with 1 heaping tablespoon of tomatoes. Garnish with shrimp and crab. Remove the liners before serving. Serve immediately after filling.

Note: This is perfect for a light luncheon.

CREOLE SHRIMP IN FILO CUPS

Serves 10

10   paper or foil muffin liners
6   ounces light cream cheese (or
     Neufchatel cheese), at
     room temperature
½   cup light sour cream
.7   ounce envelope Italian dressing
     mix
4   green onions, minced
½   cup green pepper, minced
½   pound filo leaves, thawed and
     covered with a damp
     kitchen towel

¼   cup margarine, clarified and
     melted (or ¼ cup canola
     oil with ¼ teaspoon butter
     flavoring)
10   ounces Creole-style stewed
     tomatoes, chilled
1   pound shrimp, cooked,
     peeled and chilled

Preheat oven to 350°. Put liners in 10 standard-size muffin cups.

In a medium bowl combine the Neufchatel, sour cream, Italian dressing mix, green onions, and green pepper. Mix thoroughly and refrigerate until thoroughly chilled.

Lay 3 sheets of filo on a large plastic cutting board. Using sharp scissors, or a sharp knife, cut each pastry sheet into 4 5-inch squares. Brush margarine (or canola oil) on 3 squares of filo. Place the squares on top of each other. Gently mold the 3 pastry squares into a muffin cup, leaving a 1-inch overhang. Repeat the process to form the desired number of pastry shells.

Bake at 350° for 10 minutes, or until the shells are crisp and golden brown. Place the muffin pan on a wire rack to cool for 10 minutes before filling the shells.

Carefully put 1½ tablespoons of the cream cheese filling in each shell. Top each dollop of filling with 1 heaping tablespoon of stewed tomatoes. Garnish with the shrimp. Remove the liners before serving. Serve immediately after filling.

NEUFCHATEL CHEESE AND TUNA IN FILO SHELLS

Makes 20 bite-size servings

20 3-inch squares of foil
8   ounces Neufchatel cheese (or
    cream cheese), at room
    temperature
9   ounces tuna fish packed in water,
    canned and drained
¼   cup light sour cream
½   cup fresh parsley, chopped
½   cup onion, chopped
4   ounces water chestnuts, chopped
2   tablespoons Worcestershire sauce

salt and pepper to taste
½   pound filo leaves, thawed and
    covered with a damp
    kitchen towel
¼   cup margarine, clarified and
    melted (or ¼ cup canola
    oil with ¼ teaspoon butter
    flavoring)

Preheat oven to 350°. Line 20 miniature muffin cups with foil squares.

In a medium mixing bowl combine the Neufchatel, tuna fish, sour cream, parsley, and onion. Beat with an electric mixer until thoroughly blended. Stir in the water chestnuts and Worcestershire sauce. Add salt and pepper to taste. Refrigerate until chilled.

Lay 3 sheets of filo on a large plastic cutting board. Using sharp scissors, or a sharp knife, cut each pastry sheet into 6 3-inch squares. Brush margarine (or canola oil) on squares of filo. Place the squares on top of each other. Gently mold the 3 pastry squares into a muffin cup, leaving a 1-inch overhang. Repeat the process to make the desired number of pastry shells.

Bake at 350° for 10 minutes, or until the shells are crisp and golden brown. Place the muffin pan on a wire rack to cool for 10 minutes before filling the shells.

Carefully put 1 heaping tablespoon of the cream cheese filling in each shell. Remove the foil before serving. Serve immediately after filling.

❖❖❖

STRAWBERRIES AND CHOCOLATE CREAM IN FILO CUPS

◆

Makes 8

8 paper or foil muffin liners
½ pound fresh strawberries
1 package whipped topping mix
   (approximately 1.3 ounces)
1 tablespoon cocoa powder
1½ cup 2% milk
½ teaspoon vanilla extract
½ pound filo leaves, thawed and
   covered with a damp
   kitchen towel

¼ cup margarine, clarified and
   melted (or ¼ cup canola
   oil with ¼ teaspoon butter
   flavoring)
⅓ cup almonds, (or walnuts or
   pecans), finely chopped
   (optional)

◆

Preheat oven to 350°. Put liners in 8 standard-size muffin cups.

Wash and slice the strawberries; refrigerate until needed.

Put the whipped topping mix and cocoa powder in a deep bowl. Combine thoroughly. Stir in the milk and vanilla extract. Beat with an electric mixer on high speed until thickened, about 4 minutes. Refrigerate until needed.

Lay 3 sheets of filo on a large plastic cutting board. Using sharp scissors, or a sharp knife, cut each pastry sheet into 4 5-inch squares. Brush margarine (or canola oil) on 3 squares of filo. Place the squares on top of each other. Gently mold the 3 pastry squares into a muffin cup, leaving a 1-inch overhang. Repeat the process to make the desired number of pastry shells.

Bake at 350° for 10 minutes, or until the shells are crisp and golden brown. Place the muffin pan on a wire rack to cool for 10 minutes before filling the shells.

Carefully fill the shells with the strawberries. Top with a dollop of chocolate cream. Sprinkle the nuts on top, if desired. Remove the liners before serving. Serve immediately after filling.

FRESH FRUIT IN FILO CUPS

Makes 8

8   paper or foil muffin liners
½   pound fresh fruit (or a
       combination of fruits)
      sugar (or artificial sweetener) to
       taste
½   pound filo leaves, thawed and
       covered with a damp
       kitchen towel

¼   cup margarine, clarified and
       melted (or ¼ cup canola
       oil with ¼ teaspoon butter
       flavoring)
1   cup frozen light nondairy whipped
       topping, thawed
⅓   cup almonds, walnuts, or pecans,
       finely chopped (optional)

Preheat oven to 350°. Put liners in 8 standard-size muffin cups.

Wash and cut fruit into bite-size pieces. Add sugar or sweetener as necessary.
Refrigerate until needed.

Lay 3 sheets of filo on a large plastic cutting board. Using sharp scissors, or a sharp
knife, cut each pastry sheet into 4 5-inch squares. Brush margarine (or canola
oil) on 3 squares of filo. Place the squares on top of each other. Gently mold the 3
pastry squares into a muffin cup, leaving a 1-inch overhang. Repeat the process
to form the desired number of pastry shells.

Bake at 350° for 10 minutes, or until the shells are crisp and golden brown. Place
the muffin pan on a wire rack to cool for 10 minutes before filling the shells.

Carefully fill the shells with fruit. Top with a dollop of whipped topping. Sprinkle
the nuts on top, if desired. Remove the liners before serving. Serve immediately
after filling.

Note: Other possible filling combinations include:
◆ Chocolate or vanilla ice cream with crème de menthe drizzled on top
◆ Praline ice cream with praline liquor or caramel topping drizzled on top
◆ Any pie filling topped with whipped cream or ice cream
◆ Any ice cream with your favorite sundae topping

RAISIN-PEACH CUPS

◆

Makes 8

8   paper or foil muffin liners
6   peaches
½   cup raisins
1   cup water
½   teaspoon butter flavoring
2   tablespoons brown sugar
      substitute, or to taste
2   teaspoons cornstarch
1   teaspoon cinnamon
½   pound filo leaves, thawed and
      covered with a damp
      kitchen towel

¼   cup margarine, clarified and
      melted (or ¼ cup canola
      oil with ¼ teaspoon butter
      flavoring)
    frozen light nondairy whipped
      topping

◆

Preheat oven to 350°. Put liners in 8 standard-size muffin cups.

Peel and slice the peaches. Place peaches and raisins in a medium saucepan. Add the water and butter flavoring and mix thoroughly. In a small dish, combine the brown sugar and cornstarch; stir in the cinnamon and mix thoroughly. Stir the brown sugar mixture into the peaches. Cook while stirring constantly over low heat until the peach mixture thickens. Set aside while making the shells.

Lay 3 sheets of filo on a large plastic cutting board. Using sharp scissors, or a sharp knife, cut each pastry sheet into 4 5-inch squares. Brush margarine (or canola oil) on 3 squares of filo. Place the squares on top of each other. Gently mold the 3 pastry squares into a muffin cup, leaving a 1-inch overhang. Repeat the process to make the desired number of pastry shells.

Bake at 350° for 10 minutes, or until the shells are crisp and golden brown. Place the muffin pan on a wire rack to cool.

Reheat the peaches in the saucepan over very low heat. Carefully fill the shells ¾ full with the peach filling. Top with a dollop of whipped topping. Remove the liners before serving. Serve immediately after filling.

AMBROSIA BITES IN FILO SHELLS

◆

Makes 8

8　paper or foil muffin liners
1　11-ounce can mandarin orange
　　sections, drained (or 2
　　fresh mandarin oranges, peeled
　　and seeded)
1　grapefruit, cut and seeded with
　　sections removed
½　cup coconut, grated
1　cup light sour cream
2　teaspoons artificial sweetener, or
　　to taste

½　pound filo leaves, thawed and
　　covered with a damp
　　kitchen towel
¼　cup margarine, clarified and
　　melted (or ¼ cup canola
　　oil with ¼ teaspoon butter
　　flavoring)
⅓　cup almonds (or walnuts or
　　pecans), finely chopped
　　(optional)

◆

Preheat oven to 350°. Put liners in 8 standard-size muffin cups.

Combine the orange sections, grapefruit sections, and coconut in a medium bowl. Refrigerate until needed.

Combine the sour cream and artificial sweetener. Refrigerate until needed.

Lay 3 sheets of filo on a large plastic cutting board. Using sharp scissors, or a sharp knife, cut each pastry sheet into 4 5-inch squares. Brush margarine (or canola oil) on 3 squares of filo. Place the squares on top of each other. Gently mold the 3 pastry squares in a muffin cup, leaving a 1-inch overhang. Repeat the process to make the desired number of pastry shells.

Bake at 350° for 10 minutes, or until the shells are crisp and golden brown. Place the muffin pan on a wire rack to cool for 10 minutes before filling the shells.

Carefully put about 2 tablespoons of the sour cream in each filo shell. Top with the fruit. Sprinkle a few nuts on top, if desired. Remove the liners before serving. Serve immediately after filling.

SHERBERT WITH RASPBERRY SAUCE IN FILO SHELLS

◆

Makes 8

8 paper or foil muffin liners
10 ounces frozen raspberries, thawed
2 teaspoons cornstarch
½ pound filo leaves, thawed and covered with a damp kitchen towel

¼ cup margarine, clarified and melted (or ¼ cup canola oil with ¼ teaspoon butter flavoring)
1 pint raspberry sherbert
1 cup fresh raspberries (optional)

◆

Preheat oven to 350°. Put liners in 8 standard-size muffin cups.

Drain the raspberries and save the juice. Put the raspberries through a food mill; discard the seeds. In a small saucepan, combine the raspberry juice, raspberry purèe, and cornstarch. Cook and stir constantly over low heat until smooth and thickened; set aside.

Lay 3 sheets of filo on a large plastic cutting board. Using sharp scissors, or a sharp knife, cut each pastry sheet into 4 5-inch squares. Brush margarine (or canola oil) on 3 squares of filo. Place the squares on top of each other. Gently mold the 3 pastry squares into a muffin cup, leaving a 1-inch overhang. Repeat the process to make the desired number of pastry shells.

Bake at 350° for 10 minutes, or until the shells are crisp and golden brown. Place the muffin pan on a wire rack to cool for 10 minutes before filling the shells.

Carefully fill the shells ½ full with the sherbert. Put a few fresh raspberries on top of the sherbert in each shell, if desired. Top with a couple of teaspoons of the sauce, dividing it evenly among the shells. Remove the liners before serving. Serve immediately after filling.

FRESH FRUIT AND PRALINE CREAM
IN FILO SHELLS

Makes 8

8   paper or foil muffin liners
1   package whipped topping mix
      (approximately 1.3 ounces)
⅓   cup 2% milk, very cold
1   tablespoon praline liqueur
2   nectarines
2   peaches
½   cup fresh raspberries

½   pound filo leaves, thawed and
      covered with a damp
      kitchen towel
¼   cup margarine, clarified and
      melted (or ¼ cup canola
      oil with ¼ teaspoon butter
      flavoring)
½   cup granola

Preheat oven to 350°. Put liners in 8 standard-size muffin cups.

Put the whipped topping mix, milk, and liqueur in a medium bowl, combine thoroughly. Beat on high speed with an electric mixer until fluffy and thickened, about 4 minutes. Refrigerate until needed.

Peel and slice the nectarines and peaches. Combine in a medium bowl and stir in the raspberries. Refrigerate until needed.

Lay 3 sheets of filo on a large plastic cutting board. Using sharp scissors, or a sharp knife, cut each pastry sheet into 4 5-inch squares. Brush margarine (or canola oil) on 3 squares of filo. Place the squares on top of each other. Gently mold the 3 pastry squares into a muffin cup, leaving a 1-inch overhang. Repeat the process to make the desired number of pastry shells.

Bake at 350° for 10 minutes, or until the shells are crisp and golden brown. Place the muffin pan on a wire rack to cool for 10 minutes before filling the shells.

Drain the fruit. Carefully fill the shells ½ full with the fruit. Spoon a couple of tablespoons of the praline cream over the fruit in each shell. Top with a couple of teaspoons of granola. Remove the liners before serving. Serve immediately after filling.

SHERBERT BALLS AND FRESH FRUIT IN FILO CUPS

◆

Makes 8

8 paper or foil muffin liners
½ cantaloupe
½ honeydew melon
1 kiwi
1 cup orange sherbert
1 cup lime sherbert
½ pound filo leaves, thawed and covered with a damp kitchen towel

¼ cup margarine, clarified and melted (or ¼ cup canola oil with ¼ teaspoon butter flavoring)

◆

Preheat oven to 350°. Put liners in 8 standard-size muffin cups.

Scoop the cantaloupe and honeydew melon into small balls and place in a bowl. Peel and slice the kiwi and place in the bowl. Refrigerate until needed.

Scoop the sherbert with the melon ball scoop and place in another bowl. Freeze until needed.

Lay 3 sheets of filo on a large plastic cutting board. Using sharp scissors, or a sharp knife, cut each pastry sheet into 4 5-inch squares. Brush margarine (or canola oil) on 3 squares of filo. Place the squares on top of each other. Gently mold the 3 pastry squares into a muffin cup, leaving a 1-inch overhang. Repeat the process to make the desired number of pastry shells.

Bake at 350° for 10 minutes, or until the shells are crisp and golden brown. Place the muffin pan on a wire rack to cool for 10 minutes before filling the shells.

Carefully fill the shells half full with the sherbert. Top with the fruit. Decorate with the kiwi. Remove the liners before serving. Serve immediately after filling.

COFFEE DREAM CUPS

Makes 8

8   paper or foil muffin liners
2   packages whipped topping mix
     (approximately 1.3 ounces
     each)
½   cup 2% milk, very cold
2   tablespoons coffee-flavored
     liqueur
2   teaspoons instant coffee
2   teaspoons hot water
½   pound filo leaves, thawed and
     covered with a damp
     kitchen towel

¼   cup margarine, clarified and
     melted (or ¼ cup canola
     oil with ¼ teaspoon butter
     flavoring)
     coffee-flavored candies for
     decoration (optional)

Preheat oven to 350°. Put liners in 8 standard-size muffin cups.

Put the whipped topping mix, milk, and liqueur in a medium bowl and combine thoroughly. Beat on high speed with an electric mixer until thickened, about 4 minutes. Put the instant coffee in a small dish and stir in the hot water, continue stirring until the coffee granules dissolve. Stir the coffee into the whipped topping. Refrigerate until needed.

Lay 3 sheets of filo on a large plastic cutting board. Using sharp scissors, or a sharp knife, cut each pastry sheet into 4 5-inch squares. Brush margarine (or canola oil) on 3 squares of filo. Place the filo squares on top of each other. Gently mold the pastry squares into a muffin cup, leaving a 1-inch overhang. Repeat the process to make the desired number of pastry shells.

Bake at 350° for 10 minutes, or until the shells are crisp and golden brown. Place the muffin pan on a wire rack to cool for 10 minutes before filling the shells.

Carefully fill the shells with the coffee filling. Top with a few coffee-flavored candies, if desired. Remove the liners before serving. Serve immediately after filling.

AMARETTO AND CREAM CUPS

◆

Makes 8

8 paper or foil muffin liners
2 packages whipped topping mix (approximately 1.3 ounces each)
½ cup 2% milk, very cold
¼ cup amaretto
2 teaspoons almond extract
4 ounces light cream cheese (or Neufchatel)
½ pound filo leaves, thawed and covered with a damp kitchen towel

¼ cup margarine, clarified and melted (or ¼ cup canola oil with ¼ teaspoon butter flavoring)
½ cup almonds, chopped or ground (optional)

◆

Preheat oven to 350°. Put liners in 8 standard-size muffin cups.

Put the whipped topping mix, milk, amaretto, and almond extract in a medium bowl and combine thoroughly. Beat on high speed with an electric mixer until thickened, about 4 minutes. Beat in the cream cheese and continue beating until thickened and fluffy. Refrigerate until needed.

Lay 3 sheets of filo on a large plastic cutting board. Using sharp scissors, or a sharp knife, cut each pastry sheet into 4 5-inch squares. Brush margarine (or canola oil) on 3 squares of filo. Place the squares on top of each other. Gently mold the 3 pastry squares into a muffin cup, leaving a 1-inch overhang. Repeat the process to make the desired number of pastry shells.

Bake at 350° for 10 minutes, or until the shells are crisp and golden brown. Place the muffin pan on a wire rack to cool for 10 minutes before filling the shells.

Carefully fill the shells with the amaretto cream. Top with a few almonds, if desired. Remove the liners before serving. Serve immediately after filling.

FRESH FRUIT AND LEMON YOGURT IN FILO SHELLS

Makes 8

8   paper or foil muffin liners
½   pound fresh fruit (or a combination of assorted fruits)
½   pound filo leaves, thawed and covered with a damp kitchen towel

¼   cup margarine, clarified and melted (or ¼ cup canola oil with ¼ teaspoon butter flavoring)
1   pint frozen lemon yogurt

Preheat oven to 350°. Put liners in 8 standard-size muffin cups.

Wash and cut fruit into bite-size pieces. Refrigerate until needed.

Lay 3 sheets of filo on a large plastic cutting board. Using sharp scissors, or a sharp knife, cut each pastry sheet into 4 5-inch squares. Brush margarine (or canola oil) on 3 squares of filo. Place the squares on top of each other. Gently mold the 3 pastry squares into a muffin cup, leaving a 1-inch overhang. Repeat the process to make the desired number of pastry shells.

Bake at 350° for 10 minutes, or until the shells are crisp and golden brown. Place the muffin pan on a wire rack to cool for 10 minutes before filling the shells.

Carefully fill the shells ½ full with frozen yogurt. Top with fruit. Remove the liners before serving. Serve immediately after filling.

INDEX